JAN 2 0 2011

D0344467

VALLEYS OF DEATH

VALLEYS OF DEATH

A MEMOIR OF THE KOREAN WAR

COLONEL WILLIAM (BILL) RICHARDSON, U.S. ARMY (RET.)

WITH KEVIN MAURER

BERKLEY CALIBER, NEW YORK

THE BERKLEY PUBLISHING GROUP
Published by the Penguin Group
Penguin Group (USA) Inc.
375 Hudson Street, New York, New York 10014, USA
Penguin Group (Canada), 90 Eglinton Avenue East, Suite 700, Toronto, Ontario M4P 2Y3, Canada
(a division of Pearson Penguin Canada Inc.)
Penguin Books Ltd., 80 Strand, London WC2R 0RL, England
Penguin Group Ireland, 25 St. Stephen's Green, Dublin 2, Ireland (a division of Penguin Books Ltd.)
Penguin Group (Australia), 250 Camberwell Road, Camberwell, Victoria 3124, Australia
(a division of Pearson Australia Group Pty. Ltd.)
Penguin Books India Pvt. Ltd., 11 Community Centre, Panchsheel Park, New Delhi—110 017, India
Penguin Group (NZ), 67 Apollo Drive, Rosedale, North Shore 0632, New Zealand
(a division of Pearson New Zealand Ltd.)
Penguin Books (South Africa) (Pty.) Ltd., 24 Sturdee Avenue, Rosebank, Johannesburg 2196,
South Africa

Penguin Books Ltd., Registered Offices: 80 Strand, London WC2R 0RL, England

This book is an original publication of the Berkley Publishing Group.

The publisher does not have any control over and does not assume any responsibility for author or third-party websites or their content.

Copyright © 2010 by Bill Richardson
Book design by Kristin del Rosario

FIRST EDITION: December 2010

Library of Congress Cataloging-in-Publication Data

Richardson, Bill (William J.)
Valleys of death : a memoir of the Korean War / Bill Richardson & Kevin Maurer. —1st ed.
    p.   cm.
Includes index.
ISBN 978-0-425-23673-4
    1. Richardson, Bill (William J.)   2. Korean War, 1950–1953—Personal narratives, American.
3. Korean War, 1950–1953—Prisoners and prisons.   4. Prisoners of war—Korea (North)—Biography.
5. Prisoners of war—United States—Biography.   6. Soldiers—United States—Biography.
I. Maurer, Kevin.   II. Title.
DS921.6.R53 2010
951.904'27—dc22
[B]   2010017349

PRINTED IN THE UNITED STATES OF AMERICA

10 9 8 7 6 5 4 3 2 1

This story is dedicated to the combat infantrymen who fought and died so heroically from the Pusan Perimeter to Unsan, North Korea.
And to those who died and survived the horrors of prison camps in North Korea.
And to my wife, Claire, with all my love.
Without her this story would never have been written.

ACKNOWLEDGMENTS

Over the years a number of individuals have contributed to bringing this story to fruition. I will forever be indebted to the following:

David Halberstam for his friendship and encouragement on the writing of this book. It was sad that his untimely death took place just as his latest book, *The Coldest Winter*, was published.

Thomas Richardson, my brother who conducted the research in the National Archives of the Eighth Cavalry Regiment actions in Korea up to the battle of Unsan. His research confirmed the timeline and actions I had placed in my initial drafts.

Richard Boylan, chief of the U.S. Government Military Archives for assisting my brother and helping to locate my dossier of the debrief on my return from North Korea.

To my friends in the Department of Defense, MIA-POW, Dan Baughman, Philip O'Brien and the rest of the outstanding personnel for their help over the years.

Tim Casey, CSM retired, for his friendship and correspondence over the years. He has been a reservoir of knowledge on U.S. Korean POWs.

My niece Nancy Richardson Patchan, for the editing of my work on the first attempt at writing.

CONTENTS

CONTENTS

PREFACE

This is not a history of the Korean War. It is a down and dirty look at some of the soldiers who, five years before, had experienced combat in the second world war. It is the story of the men they would lead, a new generation of courageous young soldiers in what would be the last true Infantry war.

The heroes of this story are the young men of the Third Battalion, Eighth Cavalry Regiment and in particular the men of the weapons platoon of "L" Company. Most of them died in combat or in the horrible conditions of a prison in North Korea.

The story is told through my own eyes. I have made a strong attempt to avoid adding to the story what others have said or what I have learned over the last fifty-seven years. But there are a few truths that are undeniable.

Korea was a war that neither the country nor the military was ready for, and we paid a high price for our lack of readiness. The disaster at Unsan written about in this book was caused by a lapse of leadership from the highest echelon down to the battalion level. Mistakes we paid for with the blood of the most heroic men I have ever known.

Some may ask why I waited so long to write the story. Although my experience in Korea guided my career through the years, I never felt that it was any more than a unique experience that very few men had.

Also, while I will never forget Korea, some of the details were buried deep in the recesses of my mind, much like the weapons platoon rosters I buried by a bridge abutment in North Korea. No matter how much I try, I cannot recall many of the names in my unit. For one, many were replacements whom I met in the midst of combat. Also during the thirty-four months in prison, survival was paramount in my mind. Therefore, I could not provide every soldier's name or recall his upbringing or his hometown. Over the years the loss of men's names is the one thing that has haunted me and caused me a great deal of sadness. I can still see their faces and they are men that will be with me forever, even without names.

Ten years ago, I was given the opportunity to share my experience with young Special Forces soldiers who were participating in a three-week course on survival, evasion, resistance, and escape (SERE). It was through this program that I met a young reporter, Kevin Maurer, who was writing a story on the SERE program. He heard me speak and later asked if he could write an article about me for the *Fayetteville Observer*. I agreed and he wrote a great story. This was the beginning of a friendship.

It was shortly after that I asked Kevin if he would consider collaborating on a book. I needed him to break me of my military style of writing. He was continuously after me to tell the story the way I did when I spoke to the soldiers. In turn, I had to educate him on the Korean War, our equipment, organization, and the language we used back in the day. When I was young I liked to associate with older people. Now that I am considered old I like to be with younger people. Our relationship worked well.

During the production and publication of this book, my young friend and coauthor Kevin went back to Afghanistan to write about the new Greatest Generation—the less than 1 percent of our great nation's youth who are sacrificing their lives in order that the other 99 percent of us can enjoy our freedom. Kevin will, much like Ernie Pyle, put a face on these young warriors.

So here is the story, the good, the bad and the ugly.

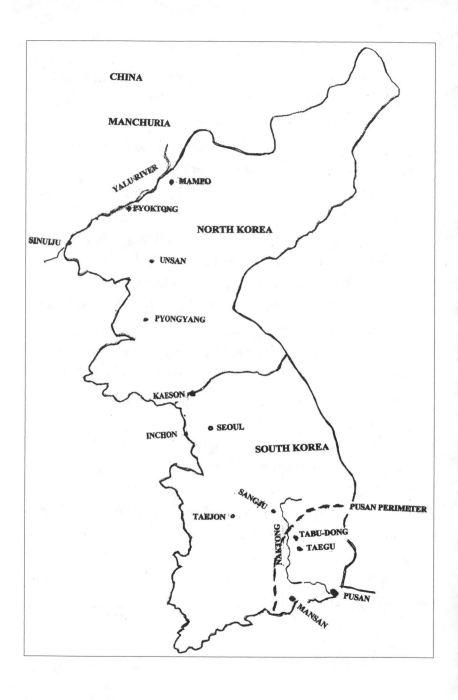

CHAPTER ONE

WAR

The world looked just great before the morning of June 25, 1950.

That morning, halfway around the world, under a dismal rainy sky, the North Korean Army crossed the 38th parallel, overwhelming the South Korean Army and sending them running south. I was home on leave in Philadelphia. I'd spent the last four years in Italy, Germany and finally Austria, on occupation duty with the U.S. Army. At my mother's house in Philadelphia, the radio kept a steady stream of updates. Outside at the newsstand, the headlines screamed off the page.

REDS INVADE SOUTH KOREA!

ARTILLERY SMASHES INTO SOUTH KOREAN TOWNS AS TANKS STREAM ACROSS THE 38TH PARALLEL!

KOREAN REFUGEES STREAM SOUTH IN FRONT OF THE NORTH KOREAN ONSLAUGHT!

Meeting in emergency session, the U.N. Security Council voted to defend South Korea. The Soviets were boycotting over the U.N.'s refusal to recognize Communist China. The U.N. put the United States in charge and named General Douglas MacArthur the commander of U.N. forces. This would be the U.N.'s first war.

Fifty-three countries registered their support, and twenty-two of them offered troops and other help. But the United States would carry the main military load—something it wasn't prepared to do.

That night, President Truman told the nation that he was committing U.S. forces to Korea. I reported for duty at the replacement center at Fort Devens, Massachusetts. There were a number of men waiting to be discharged. It had been the same scene when I reported to Fort Dix, New Jersey, a few weeks earlier.

At Fort Dix I was standing in line at the replacement center, a hastily built wooden building created to house troops during World War II, with transfer papers in hand. I watched man after man get his discharge. I didn't want to get out and hoped to get an extension. I'd met a girl in Austria and hoped to get back over to Europe with a new unit.

After an hour, I made it to the front. A sergeant in a crisp uniform, with chestnut hair, stared up from her small desk. She wasn't bad looking, but she had a lethal demeanor, like a cobra ready to strike.

"Name, rank, serial number," she snapped.

"Corporal William J. Richardson, RA13150752."

She looked down at my personnel file and then back at me.

"Corporal, we are discharging you for the convenience of the government."

The words hit me like a hammer. I stood there stunned and muttering.

"What? I've got more than four months on my extension."

Then I got mad.

"Goddamn it, I don't want to be discharged"

She looked up again. Her eyes narrow. Angry.

"Well goddamn it, you're going to be. Like it or not," she snapped back.

I swallowed my anger and took a deep breath. I knew I wasn't going to argue my way back into the Army.

"Hey, Sarge, I'm sorry I came on so strong. Look, I really

want to stay in," I said, trying to be sincere. "I sure would like to have the rest of my time to figure out what I want to do when I reenlist."

I smiled sheepishly. I really needed the remaining time on my extension to determine how I was going to get back to Austria or how I was going to get Rose, my girlfriend, over to the States. Rose and I met when she was a domestic working for two officers' families in my unit, and I hadn't thought of much else since I'd left.

"Come on, please. Give me a break."

The sergeant stopped writing in my file and looked up at me. Sweeping a lock of chestnut hair out of her eyes, she stared at me like she was trying to see through my facade. Was I full of shit? I hated that coldhearted bitch, but I held on to my smile until my cheeks hurt.

Finally, she smiled.

"All right, damn it. I'm going to reassign you to Fort Devens," she said.

Where the hell was that? I almost asked for Fort Dix, but I held my tongue.

"Gee, Sarge, that's great. Thanks."

I made it to the replacement center at Fort Devens, Massachusetts, a few days after the North Korean invasion. That night, President Truman issued an executive order extending everyone for one year. He was going to make a stand against Communism in Korea. Only a few of the soldiers in line were there to be assigned to a unit. Most wanted to get discharged, especially with the news coming out of Korea, but they were now being assigned to new units. Units that were likely headed to Korea.

Everyone thought it would be over quickly though. Hell, we didn't even really care about Korea. When Secretary of State Dean Acheson had highlighted American interests in the Pacific a few years before, he didn't even mention the Korean Peninsula. That turned out to be an invitation to North Korea, backed by Russia and China, to test their expansion desires. We didn't leave tanks there after World War II since the terrain was not suitable, a fact the North Koreans dismissed when they crashed into South Korea with their Russian-made T-34 tanks.

The next morning ten of us were in the parking lot joking and laughing about all the other guys being extended. Who, by the way, were pissed.

The joking and laughter stopped when a deuce-and-a-half truck pulled into the dusty parking lot. We piled on and were taken to the Third Battalion, Seventh Regiment, Third Division headquarters. It was a typical old World War II building with white wooden slats. I handed my file to a sergeant who put me in L Company. The commander wanted to speak to us at the base theater. I figured it was a normal welcome brief. I got to the theater with a few minutes to spare. The lights went down and I settled into my second row seat.

"THIS IS THE INFANTRY" splashed across the screen.

For the next eleven minutes I sat through a World War II film showing scenes of men charging enemy positions with bayonets gleaming in the sunlight. The next scene showed soldiers racing through artillery fire with rifles in hand. Finally, they were on a hill recapturing one of the Aleutian Islands from the Japanese. The action faded to a final scene: a company of soldiers standing ramrod straight in formation as an officer pinned medals on their chests.

"For every man that is decorated for bravery another five go unrecognized but proudly wear the Combat Infantryman's Badge," the narrator boomed.

A picture of the badge, with its long musket flanked by a U-shaped oak wreath, flashed on the screen before it faded to black.

Just as the lights came up, Lieutenant Colonel Harold K. Johnson stepped in front of the screen. A slight man with short-cropped gray hair, he wasn't overly impressive but had an air of authority.

"You men already wearing the Combat Infantryman's Badge will soon be wearing a star on it," he told us. "And the rest of you will be wearing the badge. We've been ordered to Korea and will be leaving in two weeks."

I looked around me and there were only two or three rows occupied. There weren't enough men to make a good company let alone a battalion. But Johnson went right on talking as if he were oblivious to that fact.

"There's a lot to be done in a very short period of time and there's no time to waste. It's going to be action packed," he said. "May God bless you all."

There was a great silence as we filed out of the old theater. As we walked back, a young sergeant who had been sitting next to me finally broke the tension.

"God, I just got married and I'm on CQ tonight."

"I'll take your duty tonight. I just got here and have nothing to do," I said, introducing myself. Charge of Quarters, or CQ in Army lingo, is usually pretty boring. You answer phones and make sure the barracks don't burn down. It is like a nighttime front desk job.

"Sergeant Roberts," he said, shaking my hand. "Are you sure?"

"Yeah, I'm sure."

For a second I thought he was going to hug me. Back at the company we got clearance from the first sergeant and I took over the duty for the night. I settled into the desk that evening. My mind started to wander back to my last few weeks at home.

After getting my transfer to Fort Devens a month ago, I'd grabbed the last bus to Philadelphia. Sliding a scrap of paper with my mother's new address on it out of my pocket, I climbed into a cab at the bus station. I'd never been to the new house before. She'd moved soon after I left for Europe.

My sister Dottie had sent me the new address with a letter a couple of months ago. She'd also sent a picture. I didn't recognize her at first and knew I wouldn't recognize my other three siblings either. They'd all grown up since I'd been gone.

I got to the house just before midnight. It was one of a dozen two-story row houses. I jumped out of the cab, tossing a few bucks to the driver, snatched my duffel bag from the seat and ran up the old white steps. It was late, so there were no lights on in the house. I banged on the door and rang the doorbell.

No answer.

All of a sudden three heads popped out of the second-floor window.

"Who's there? What do you want?"

"It's Bill," I said. Neither my brother nor my sisters recognized me.

All of a sudden a little head popped up between the other three. It was my youngest brother, Tom.

"It's our brother Billy, go down and let him in."

All four came down and opened the front door. I was shocked by what I saw. I had been their big brother and took care of them, but now two of them were teenagers, Dottie and Jean; John was twelve and almost a teenager.

Tommy, the youngest, marched out onto the stoop and helped me with my bag. He seemed to remember me more than the others. We sat around the kitchen table and I fixed myself a ham and cheese on rye bread and had a beer. While I was eating, they were talking a mile a minute.

"How long will you be home?" Dottie asked.

"Do you have a picture of your girlfriend?" Tommy asked.

I tried to keep up, but I was in awe of how much they'd changed. Dottie had always been pretty, but she'd grown into a beautiful young lady. Jean too was well on her way to being another beauty. She still had the black curly hair that had earned her the nickname "Mop Top." When I was home, I used to sing and dance for her while I was getting ready to go out. John had grown into a stocky teenager. He looked like a young Babe Ruth, and Tommy, the de facto spokesman despite being the youngest, seemed more mature than his nine years. While they were talking, I realized how much I had missed them.

My mother didn't get home until two-thirty in the morning. She had Frank, her boyfriend, in tow. I could tell they were three sheets to the wind. That was no change. My mother wouldn't stop saying how surprised she was to see me. When they walked in, I got up from the couch and hugged her. Frank stood nearby and we shook hands.

"It is good to have you back home, Billy," my mother said.

She was surprised at how much I had changed.

She was forty-three years old, but she always looked ten years younger than she was. My father and mother had been separated for five years. How it lasted as long as it did, I'll never know. She had been the life of the party for as long as I could remember.

The next day I called my father. I hadn't seen him since I'd left four years ago. We made arrangements to meet for lunch on Allegheny Avenue, outside a Horn & Hardhart restaurant. It was a famous self-serve restaurant in Philadelphia where working people could catch a quick lunch. Dad had taken me to this restaurant once or twice when I was a young kid, and I thought it was great, and here we were together and I still thought it was great. I remember I had my favorite dessert, Philadelphia cheesecake.

As I walked down the street, I saw him coming toward me. He looked a little shorter than I remembered. Before I could react or say anything, he grabbed me and right in the middle of the sidewalk, hugged and kissed me. It embarrassed the hell out of me. We went in and grabbed a table by the window. By the time we got to the Philadelphia cheesecake, we'd caught up. But when we started talking about my mother and siblings, I could see the tears well up in his eyes.

"Bill, I see Dottie once a month. She meets me on Frankford Avenue and I give her the child support money. Most of the time we just hug and cry. It's hard."

I quickly changed the subject.

"Where are you living now?" I asked.

"I'm still at Herron's house."

Bill and my dad had been partners since they were kids.

They were song-and-dance men who played all the local clubs along the eastern seaboard and on the Friehofer's radio show. My father played the banjo and Bill Herron—I called him Uncle Bill—played the marimba.

Entertainment ran in the family.

My dad's brother Frank had sung on the stage since he was eight years old. He made it to Hollywood and appeared in nine movies; *Fox Movietone Follies of 1929, Sunnyside Up* and *Happy Days*, to name a few. In 1932 my dad and Uncle Bill were scheduled to go out to Hollywood when they finished their engagement at Million Dollar Pier in Atlantic City, New Jersey. But before their last show the studio sent a telegram canceling the trip.

Frank had promised to marry a chorus girl and put it in writing. Of course he was already married, and she threatened to slap him with a million-dollar breach of promise suit. Things had caught up with him, and when it hit the headlines across the nation I had a new aunt. But the scandal stopped any interest Hollywood had in another Richardson. So my father, Bill Herron and Frank continued to play in clubs and theaters along the eastern seaboard.

In 1944 they went on tour with a show entertaining troops all across the country. In 1945, they went overseas. It was two days before I left for Europe myself. My dad arrived back home from the USO trip in Europe. My mother had her boyfriend move in, and when my dad came home she told him he was no longer welcome. We went out together and it was the first time I saw my father drink. I wanted to cry for him. My heart was breaking. I dropped him off that night at Bill Herron's house. I spent the night at my mother's house with my brothers and sisters and felt a million miles away. I loved my mother through it all, but I always felt sorry for my father.

After lunch, we went downtown to one of my dad's booking agents, checking to see if they had any shows. Dad was working at Yale & Towne as a tool crib expediter in the daytime and at nights and on weekends playing club dates.

We walked into the office and said hello to the receptionist. My father introduced me and started a pitch that I would hear with every new face about my tour overseas and how well I was doing in the Army. He was also showing me off. He was very proud of me.

Back outside, he told me he was seeing a young lady who was divorced with four children.

"She's very nice and I think you will like her, we'll get together soon," my dad said. "Hey, Bill, suppose we get together tomorrow night, go to dinner and a movie, with Cathy and me?"

"That'll be great."

The next night we went to a movie at the Earle Theater and to dinner at Bookbinders, one of Philly's best restaurants.

The one thing I remember most about Cathy was she loved my dad. I saw how she snuck glances at him and how they tenderly held hands during the movie. At the end of the night, Cathy asked my dad and me if we could come to dinner at her house on Sunday. She wanted me to meet her children.

On Sunday, I pressed my uniform and met my dad at Cathy's house in northeast Philly. She had three boys, ages nine to fourteen, and a sixteen-year-old daughter, Claire. Cathy was a good cook, and she laid out a spread of roast beef, mashed potatoes and peas. In between bites, I fielded questions about

My dad and I. He had just returned from Europe and I was leaving for Europe the next day. *Author's collection.*

my travels to Italy, France and Austria. They were Catholic and marveled at my stories about the Vatican and St. Peter's Basilica.

After dinner we all went outside to take some pictures with Cathy's Kodak Brownie camera. Since Claire and I were the oldest of both families, Cathy and my dad decided we should have our picture taken together. I walked up next to her and smiled. My father told me the pictures turned out good, and it was nice to see him happy. He was the best man I have ever known.

My dad and I in June 1950, before I departed for Ft. Devens, Massachusetts. *Author's collection.*

The phone on my desk woke me from my daydream. My quiet evening was over.

"Your company will get about one hundred men in very late tonight from Fort Dix," the night officer said. "They are recruits. Right out of basic. Early in the morning we'll also be getting some troops transferred in from other outfits on post. Make sure they have a place to sleep tonight and have a hot meal for breakfast."

I hung up and called in the supply sergeant and told him to get in and be prepared to issue bed linens and blankets. Next, I called the mess sergeant and told him to come in. Finally, I requested that he have additional rations brought to the mess hall as early as possible. I called the company duty officer who was on standby and told him I thought he'd better get in.

The next few hours, I shepherded the new recruits from the buses to the mess hall, to the supply room, and then to the barracks. I didn't get a chance to sit down for a second. The next morning, when the company commander showed up to formation, we had 180 men standing in the company street.

CHAPTER TWO

FORMING THE BATTALION

I entered the company headquarters and reported to Captain Filmore McAbee.

He and First Sergeant Brien sat behind a table. They were interviewing the corporals and sergeants and giving us our assignments. The platoon leaders and platoon sergeants sat in chairs nearby.

"This is the corporal who was on duty last night, he did a great job," the first sergeant said.

McAbee, a well-built man who most likely was an athlete, was a World War II veteran. He looked up from my file and his stoic facial expression never changed.

"What experience do you have? What can you do?"

I had been a much better soldier than student. My academic

career was cut short in one brief second in my eighth-grade shop class. I was cutting up in the back of the classroom when the teacher tossed a wooden mallet at me and some friends, trying to quiet us down. The mallet hit me in the chest and fell to the floor. I stood there stunned. I didn't think. I just acted. And it cost me. I picked it up and tossed it back at the teacher. The mallet glanced off his shoulder and cracked the corner of the blackboard.

The next day, in the principal's office, it was decided that I was neither studious nor disciplined enough for high school. So I was shipped off to vocational school. World War II was raging and I got a job at a factory that produced safety glass used in bombers. Since it was defense work, we were permitted to leave school at noon to work. I made good money but knew that I didn't have a future, in school or on the factory floor.

When I wasn't working, there was always the possibility of getting into trouble. Walking in the old neighborhood with my brother Tommy while on leave, we passed a building that used to be the Italian-American Club. Seeing the old club brought back memories of how I'd conned some money from Louie, some wannabe wiseguy who wanted us to steal some hubcaps for him.

We were hanging out down the street when he came out and called me over. He pointed to his car across the street and told me he needed two hubcaps. I went back and told my friends, who wanted to go see a movie. There was a lot of bullshit talk. The truth was nobody was very up to stealing hubcaps, but with the money we could all see a movie.

I thought it over and grabbed a friend.

"Let's look at the other side of his car."

I thought there were two hubcaps on his car and figured we could take them off and sell them to him.

"Goddamn, Bill, he will kill us when he finds out," my friend said.

"Yeah, but we'll all be at the movies by the time he finds out."

I popped the hubcaps off and took them across the street to the club. Louie came out, took one look at the hubcaps, and smiled.

"Well, that's fast work," Louie said. "How about you put them on?"

I hotfooted it across the street, put the hubcaps on and headed to the movies. A few days later, I was walking down the street and Louie grabbed me. Luckily a bunch of guys from the club were there and they were laughing at him and told him to let me go.

"The kid outsmarted you, let him go."

Louie shook me by my collar and then shoved me.

"You little son of a bitch, get out of here."

That summer, I decided I needed to get out of Philadelphia. I was not quite sixteen years old when my uncle pulled some strings and got me into the War Department, with the North Atlantic Division of the U.S. Army Corps of Engineers. My mother agreed and I was signed on as a deckhand on a ship berthed out of Wilmington, Delaware. I was on the ship for a year. The war ended and the War Department was reducing its strength. My mother signed a waiver so that I could join the regular Army. A few days later, I was on a train headed south to Fort Belvoir, Virginia, for three weeks of training. I loved the military and quickly fell into the routine. The structure and discipline kept me in check, and since I was a good athlete— I'd made the varsity baseball team as a freshman in vocational school—I excelled during the long runs and dozens of push-ups. I learned quickly that keeping my head down, listening and refusing to give up were the secrets to success in the Army.

I didn't realize that I had passed my entrance exam high enough that they had me take the Officer Candidate Test. I passed it but wasn't old enough to be considered. Instead, I finished up my training and shipped out to Italy.

I had been an instructor for two years at a noncommissioned officers school in Austria and had trained and led a provisional Ranger platoon. I knew unit tactics and every weapon inside and out.

"Sir, I can do any job in this company."

The words shocked me as soon as I spit them out. McAbee smiled and glanced over to the first sergeant. McAbee was an experienced officer from World War II and knew what combat was like and knew he needed experienced sergeants to lead the way.

"Give me the characteristics of the M-1 rifle."

I didn't hesitate.

"Thirty-caliber rifle, gas-operated, bolt action, semiautomatic, clip-fed, muzzle velocity twenty-eight hundred feet per second, weight 9.5 pounds. Can be fitted with an M-7 grenade launcher placed into the barrel, with an M-15 sight mounted just forward of the trigger housing."

Soon, I was under verbal fire. The faster I answered, the faster the next question came at me.

"What are the characteristics of the BAR?"

"Browning automatic rifle, weight twenty pounds, gas-operated, muzzle velocity 2,798 feet per second, effective range one hundred to fifteen hundred yards, max range forty-five hundred to five thousand yards, fed with a twenty-round magazine."

It went on and on for ten minutes. They thought I was a smart-ass. Then all of a sudden the first sergeant stopped and looked at Captain McAbee.

"Goddamn it, I think he's for real," Brien said.

The captain nodded and asked the final question.

"How well do you know the 57 recoilless rifle?"

"Sir," I said, "very well."

McAbee knew the road ahead. He had a bunch of raw recruits it was his responsibility to prepare for battle.

"Well, you're the 57 section leader, and you have very few days to train men that don't know the front end of the weapon from the ass end," McAbee said. "Lieutenant Winn, he's yours."

Winn, the weapons platoon leader, smiled and made a note on his roster. I didn't see much of Lieutenant Winn after I took over. He was quiet and not very aggressive. I really didn't know how much he knew about the 57 recoilless rifles or the 60 mortars, so it was easier for him to stay out of the way.

McAbee dismissed me, and Winn took me out and introduced me to Sergeant First Class Albert Vaillancourt, the weapons platoon sergeant, and Sergeant First Class Gordon Roberts, the mortar section leader. I already knew Roberts. He'd just been married and I'd taken his CQ shift.

Vaillancourt had seen combat in Burma with Merrill's Marauders in World War II. He was married and had three children. One of the children was only two months old. Vaillancourt knew what to expect. He'd fought deep in the triple canopy jungles. They had to use machetes to cut through the bush, which was so thick, it would block out the sunlight. It was always hot and humid. It felt like hell, he said. But he heard the landscape in Korea was different. It could be extremely hot all day and then turn bitter cold. A different kind of hell, Vaillancourt told me.

He was reluctant to talk about combat and I didn't press him.

A few nights later the sergeants were scheduled to go on a night compass course. Some of the men in the weapons platoon were headed to town. I told them to wait for me, I would be back in a couple of hours. This brought a chorus of laughter.

"You are full of crap, you'll be out there for four or five hours," said one of the men.

I was paired with Roberts. Since we were section leaders, we worked closely together. Roberts had limited World War II experience and wasn't thrilled about heading off to war again. He knew he would miss his new wife. He wanted to be home right now with a regular life—a house, a good job and a few kids—not struggling through the woods looking for random points in the dark. I wanted to go out. As the other pairs prepared to hustle into the woods, I pulled Roberts aside.

"Do you want to get home to your wife quickly?"

"Sure, but how are we going to do that?" he asked.

"Get the map out on the ground and cover us with a poncho."

We got under the poncho with a flashlight, and I told him we were not going to walk through the woods. We were going to shoot the azimuth on the map, get the distance, see where it intersected with a terrain feature, a road or creek, and take the quickest way to that point. To make this work, you had to know how to figure the change in the magnetic declination on the map.

I shot the azimuth, made the change and traced it with my finger along the map until I hit a trail or road intersection.

"There," I said, getting up and folding the poncho and putting it over my pistol belt.

We hustled down the road and ducked down a trail and made it to the stake well before the others. We did the same thing at each stake we found. An hour and a half later we made it to the last stake. The captain waiting to certify all the teams was shocked to see us. Some teams were just getting to the first and second point. But we had all the stake numbers correct.

"I don't know how the shit you did it, but you are finished."

We just smiled and punched each other in the arm. I joined the guys and went to town; Roberts went home.

Since I was the ranking weapons platoon noncommissioned officer living in the barracks, I was responsible for keeping the barracks clean and orderly. It was a typical World War II–era barracks. An aisle ran down the middle, with folding cots on both sides. Each of us had a small shelf and clothes rack on the wall at the head of the cot and a footlocker at the foot. We had plenty of room for equipment and uniforms. In those days, civilian clothing wasn't authorized.

During my first few days with the company, I realized why I'd been put in a senior position. Our army was hollow. The Army was in bad shape, including divisions with only two battalions in their regiments instead of three. We had reduced the size of the Army so much since the end of World War II that we didn't have enough troops, equipment or leaders to go to war again.

My fifteen-man section were mostly raw recruits. When I asked how many had any experience beyond basic training, only four hands went up. The entire force was moving sergeants from one unit to another trying to get them to the units as they were being deployed. The initial rush to bring a few divisions to strength left the follow-on divisions and units basically with all new sergeants and men.

Looking at my roster, I assigned Corporal James Walsh to lead one squad. He was about five feet, eleven inches tall and about 150 pounds, a wiry guy from New York; his father owned a bar in Brooklyn and he spoke with a thick accent. Being city boys from the East Coast, we bonded quickly. We were both brash and had that quiet cockiness about us. I guess that's why we were so close right from the start.

A Yankees fan, Walsh used to listen to games on the radio with me in the barracks. The Phillies were a young team and I had a good feeling that they'd meet the Yanks in the series. Or at least that is what I kept telling Walsh.

"If you guys make it, you ain't got a chance," he told me. "The Phillies? How they gonna beat the Yankees?"

He talked for hours about Brooklyn, how he would play stickball in the streets late into the summer nights. Much like we did in Philadelphia.

My other squad leader, Corporal Walter Gray, was a little older and quieter, a good guy.

Corporal Robert Hall had been around a little and seemed like he was going to be good. I made him the gunner in Walsh's squad.

Scanning the rest of my roster, I stopped on Private First Class William Heaggley. He was also from Philadelphia. His parents owned a small neighborhood bakery.

But looking at his awards, I saw he'd recently won the Expert Infantryman's Badge. No small feat. The test is a very comprehensive look at every facet of what a top-notch infantryman should know, ranging from first aid and weapons to tactics. Out of a seven hundred–man battalion, only about ten to fifteen passed. Right off the bat, I knew Heaggley would be one of my best men.

He was the quiet type—a yes-or-no kind of guy. He was real shy, which made him even more valuable. It was good to bullshit when you were in the barracks, but in the field you had to be all business. Heaggley was all business with an eagle eye.

I would have liked to have made Heaggley a squad leader, but rank prevented that.

I had two young kids, Greenlowe and Jones. I didn't think either one of them was seventeen. Greenlowe was a nice young guy who listened to what he was told. Jones on the other hand was a smart-ass I knew I was going to have to watch.

Corporal Charles King from the mortar section was also in the barracks. King was a big Midwestern boy from Indiana with whom not too many people would want to tangle. You could tell he worked out—he had big muscular forearms like steel beams and a perfect back for carrying equipment in the field. And he was outgoing. He had a deep, infectious laugh.

He and I became good friends along with Walsh, Hall and Heaggley. Looking back, I realize we were a great crew. We were so optimistic and full of life. We talked about how this would be a short war and how we would all hang out when we returned.

"One day I'm going to take you-all down to New Orleans," King told us.

"Mardi gras, you haven't lived until you've seen Mardi gras."

"Yeah, well, you ain't lived until you see Yankee Stadium," Walsh said.

As close as you become with one another—a brotherlike bond—I really knew very little about the others' pasts. In my case, the men of the section were together a very short time. Some were gone within days; others lasted a little longer. I knew Walsh the longest, but that was only four months. If you'd asked me how well I knew Walsh then, I'd have told you I knew him like a brother. But as the years pass, I realize I knew very little of his life before our friendship.

The 57 was a fairly new weapon to the Army's inventory, so we had a good supply of guns, ammo and parts. But few soldiers knew how to use it. Luckily, I'd taught it in Austria. Essentially, it was a lightweight breech-loaded gun developed after World War II to punch holes in tanks, bunkers and buildings. Capable of firing artillery-type shells without recoil, the weapon was effective in killing Soviet-style T-34 tanks and light enough that it could be fired from the shoulder, on a tripod, or in a jeep.

The colonel had us run wearing our field gear, helmet, pack and ammo belt everywhere we went. In Korea, we'd have gun jeeps and ammo trailers, but my men all needed strong legs and backs. The 57 recoilless rifle weighed forty-five pounds and the ammo weighed six pounds per round. We also needed to carry .30-caliber ammo for our rifles and grenades. If we needed to hump the guns and ammo up and down hills, we had to be ready.

We had a very limited time to train, so Colonel Johnson had us concentrate on battle drills. We found out that Johnson had been captured on Bataan during World War II and remained a prisoner for over three years before being released. Because of Bataan, he was less trusting and understood the harshness of war.

The battalion spent time on the range shooting every rifle and machine gun in the arsenal. On the grenade range, instead of the normal sandbag pit, we ran up, threw the grenades and hit the prone position to mimic real-life combat conditions.

Johnson knew that in Korea we wouldn't have the protection of the pit. One man, I'm not sure from which company, didn't get down fast enough and shrapnel caught him in the leg. We could see the blood as he rolled on the ground moaning. The medics put him on a litter and carried him over to a waiting ambulance. Everybody was hollering at him as they put him in the ambulance.

"Million-dollar wound," they all chanted.

When we weren't shooting, we spent time getting shot at. And in retrospect, it was great training for the hell we would face on the battlefield.

Colonel Johnson marched us out on the range and had the 3.5 mortars and artillery fire five hundred yards downrange. Then he walked the battalion to within a hundred yards of the exploding shells. Everything I'd heard about the colonel proved to be true. He was tough and knew what it was going to take to put a green unit together so it had a chance of survival in combat. I could feel the earth shake. The force of the explosions was like punches to the chest. Afterward, we staggered off a little dazed. Johnson was certainly doing everything he could to get us ready.

One day we were practicing crew drills in the company area. It is similar to practicing football plays. The squad leader identifies a target, direction, distance and what type of round to be fired, while the crew prepares the weapon to fire. Quick, sharp and concise. We'd gotten it down to several seconds between rounds, but the goal was to repeat it to the point that it became muscle memory. It had to be that way because in combat, we'd have to do it under fire.

During a short smoke break, a runner came and told me that the colonel was walking through the company and checking barracks. Shit. I had two cases of beer and a case of soda in the shower, with the cold water running on them so they would be cool when we finished training. Alcohol was not permitted in the barracks and I was wasting water. I ran to the barracks and arrived just in time.

"Sir, Corporal Richardson, weapons platoon. I'm the barracks noncommissioned officer, follow me, sir."

He nodded and followed me through the door and into the barracks. As we walked, Johnson scanned the room and asked me about the platoon.

"Your men ready for Korea?"

"They're training hard and we'll be ready, sir."

We turned the corner and I could hear the shower running over the cans. I was prepared to take my ass-chewing like a man.

"Sir, I've got some drinks in the shower trying to keep them cool for the men."

He looked at the shower and turned to me.

"That's good, Corporal, the barracks look good," Johnson said. "Use every minute you can to get your men ready."

CHAPTER THREE

MOVEMENT TO THE FAR EAST

On August 4, eight trucks sat idling at the end of the street.

Men mingled in crisp green fatigues and full field gear, helmets, weapons and packs. A melancholy cloud hung over the whole company area. A few men clutched their wives and girlfriends like drowning men clutch a life raft. I stood with the single guys, smoking and telling jokes near the back of the formation.

I was anxious to get going. Hurry up and wait. One of the first things you learn about the Army.

I saw Roberts. He was hugging his beautiful young wife— tall, slim and graceful. I knew a lot of us envied him that day. She was the kind of woman that most of us hoped to come home to when the war was over.

Finally, the first sergeant came out of the orderly room and moved to his position in the company street. Immediately the platoon sergeants called their platoons to attention. There was a gravity to it. We were on the doorstep of war. We all knew it and wanted to be disciplined because when the bullets started, discipline could be the difference between life and death. The company formed, the platoon sergeants made their reports.

"All present and accounted for."

We all stood ramrod straight, our rifles at our sides. The first sergeant, company roster in hand, started calling each man's name.

"Corporal Richardson, William."

"Present," I loudly responded.

It felt good to release some of the tension. We were going off to war, and most of us, including me, had no idea what we were about to face. After calling out all 172 names, each one answered, the first sergeant turned and reported to McAbee.

"All present, sir."

McAbee gave the command to "post."

The first sergeant and the platoon sergeants moved to the back of the formation. There was a quietness that surrounded everything. A sort of finality. Seconds later, the order was given to board the trucks. We rode to the railhead in silence. Roberts just sat looking out of the truck, back to where he'd left his wife.

At the railhead the battalion was loaded on three trains for the three-and-a-half-day trip to California. They were World War II olive-drab cars. Each train was made up of two baggage cars, one kitchen car and several sleeper coaches. One baggage car was used to accommodate the company's field mess equipment. This is where our meals would be prepared and distributed while we crossed the country.

Seats in the daytime converted to an upper and lower bunk at night and at one end of the coach there was a bathroom capable of handling six to ten men at a time. It was pretty damn nice. There was only one thing missing—beer. We'd barely been on the rails for a day before King convinced a civilian at one of the stations to get us some cases of beer.

We put it in the bathroom sinks to keep cool. By the time we got to Pennsylvania, the order came down banning beer. That didn't stop us. The trick was to hide it so the officers could not find it. Each coach had two or three water coolers mounted to the wall and the porters helped us hide the beer in the bottom of the cabinet that held up the tank.

I watched as America sped across my window, marveling at how much it had changed since I'd been gone. I remembered my first train ride after getting back from Austria. I was with three hundred other soldiers heading home fresh from occupation duty. I was on my way to Fort Dix, New Jersey, to process my orders and be assigned to a new unit.

Squeezing down the aisle in the middle of the train, I found a seat near the back of the car. The train crept out of the station and was soon barreling down the track. Looking out of the window, I noticed metal lightning rods on the roofs of the houses. They seemed to sprout out of the roofs like weeds.

"When did they start putting lightning rods on all the houses?"

The soldier next to me looked out the window and shook his head. "What are you talking about?"

I pointed to the rooftops and they all started to laugh.

"They're not lightning rods," the guy said. "They are television antennas."

I shook my head in disbelief. "You mean to tell me that all those people have televisions?"

"How long have you been gone?" the soldier asked me.

I laughed at the memory as the train pulled into a town near Chicago. Each stop, we all filed off and did jumping jacks, push-ups and sit-ups on the platform. Civilians, waiting for a train, stood off to the side and watched. Some of the men, probably World War II veterans, wanted to know where we were going and wished us luck. They knew what was in store. As the train pulled out of the station, they cheered. We were off to war. Off to fight the first battle against Communism.

But there was little to cheer about in the papers and on the radio. We followed the war closely as we traveled. Every stop, besides beer, we got the latest papers, and the radio was on all day. The reports from the front were sobering.

The war in Korea had reached crisis level. American and South Korean units were fighting for their lives. They'd been swept from the 38th parallel and quickly forced out of Seoul. The North Koreans swept south toward Pusan, a port on the eastern tip of the Korean Peninsula. Now our troops were making their last stand along the Naktong River in the west and a line north of Taegu reaching east to the sea of Japan. It was bad and we knew it.

King, usually boisterous and chatty, was quiet as soon as we crossed into Indiana.

He had just returned from Okinawa and had not been able to take a leave. We were scheduled to go through Indiana very close to his hometown. He was struggling with himself over whether to get off the train and go home. It wasn't that he was scared to go to Korea. He was just not sure he could go to war without seeing his family. What if he never came back? No one said it. We didn't have to. We all knew and wouldn't blame him if he got off the train. You could see him debating in his head. Finally, he got up from staring out the window and pulled me aside.

"Make sure I don't do something stupid."

He was an awfully big guy, so I alerted three guys I thought could handle him. I told them when we got near his hometown I wanted them to be prepared to stop him if I gave them the signal. In the meantime, I kept a cold beer in his hand at all times. He only made it through a few hands of poker that night before he was snoring at the back of the car. When he woke up the next morning, we were well past his home.

After three days, we pulled into Camp Stoneman, California. Located forty miles northeast of San Francisco, the camp was named after a cavalry commander during the Civil War. Activated in 1942, during World War II it became the primary jumping off point for more than one million American soldiers destined for the Pacific. Now it was the first stop on the way to Korea.

As I looked out over the camp, it was stark and barren and probably hadn't changed since 1942. At the railhead, we got on trucks that took us to us to a row of khaki-colored World War II transit barracks. As in the barracks at Fort Devens, we settled into rows of double-decked cots. We were crammed in like sardines because there were two more infantry battalions, a couple of artillery battalions and an anti-aircraft battalion also at the camp. All of us were headed for Korea on the same ship.

After chow that night, we started looking for something to do. The camp boasted three movie theaters and eight small post exchanges, which stocked stationery, toilet articles, tobacco, candy, ice cream and beer. There was one USO building. King, Walsh, Hall, Heaggley and I found a large club. By nine o'clock, the club was packed. We found a table, and the waitress was busy and happy to see us in good spirits.

"The last guys through here were depressed and sad. You boys have spirit, like you're off to save the world," she said.

The club wasn't prepared for this many men and soon ran out of beer. So ended the night.

The next morning, Colonel Johnson had the whole battalion up and in full field gear for a forced march in the blazing hot California sun.

"Lets go, men," I said as I policed up my section.

King did the same with the mortar section.

"You look like shit, Rich," he said.

"I look like you feel," I said.

There were a lot of asses dragging on the march. I did my best to keep my men moving. It was easy for me to keep up. I didn't have a choice. I had to set the example. But I felt like dragging ass too.

We were only there for three days. Boredom was the biggest enemy, and soon some of the guys started to talk about going into town. The only problem was we were restricted to the post.

"How about we do a night training exercise," I said.

"What, like a patrol or something?" King asked.

I smiled. "Right. We'll go on patrol and break out of camp."

King jumped on the idea and started to egg me on. By that evening, I'd told Walsh and Heaggley to cover for me. If they were asked, I was somewhere on post but they didn't know where. Shortly after dark I was leading a patrol formation across an open field toward the camp fence. We made our way through the fence and moved down a side road to an intersection, where we found a cabstand.

We got into three cabs and headed for Vallejo. We called it Valley Jo. After several rounds in the local bars, King and some of the guys from the mortar section wanted to go over to the whorehouse. Most had never been and wanted to take advantage before we shipped out.

The cabbie knew exactly where to go.

We pulled up to a large, well-kept three-story Victorian house in the middle of town. Inside, the parlor had a bar and a piano player just like the movies. The girls, all nice-looking, were dressed in lacy underwear and silky robes. They were mingling with a few civilians when we arrived. Our uniforms immediately attracted their attention and they moved toward us like bees toward honey.

Two or three of the guys got hooked up with girls and went upstairs. I wasn't interested from the beginning, but I didn't want the guys to think that I didn't like women. I just had a girlfriend waiting in Austria.

I took a seat and got a beer. One of the girls that didn't get picked came over and sat on the chair. She was nice-looking, but had hard eyes. She rubbed my arm and smiled.

"So, you going to Korea?"

I smiled. "I'm sorry. I'm not interested."

She laughed and kept stroking my arm. "That's okay. I just want to talk. Are you worried about dying?"

At this point I didn't really want to discuss it with a stranger. Before I could answer, I heard a crash upstairs and a lot of yelling. Then one of the mortar men came banging down the stairs. He was mad and kept screaming about how he wanted his money back.

I got up and met King at the stairs. His shirt was open and his hair a mess, but he couldn't stop laughing.

"Seems he is hung like a donkey and the ladies don't want none," King said.

"Get him out of here before he does something stupid," I said, trying to shepherd donkey boy to the door.

King dragged him out. I rounded up the others, none too pleased to leave before they got the full service. We jumped in the cabs and headed back to camp. I saw King behind the wheel of one and got the cabs to stop. I threw open the door to King's cab.

"Get your big ass out of there. What the hell do you think you are doing?" I asked.

"Shit, Rich, I'm only having a little fun," he said.

"Your fun is going to get us all in trouble. Get out now!" I barked.

"Okay, I'm sorry Rich, you don't have to get mad," he said as he fell out of the cab.

We arrived outside the camp and slipped through the fence and across the field. It was our last night of fun. A final taste of America.

The next day we boarded a ferry that took us over to where the U.S. troop transport *Pope* was docked. The *Pope* had just been taken out of mothballs, and the ventilation system on board was not working. It was a miserably hot day. Everybody was wringing wet with sweat, which got worse the deeper we climbed into the ship.

The troop compartment space was a cavernous room with bunks four high, accommodating forty to eighty men. We stowed our gear and had started to go up to the deck, when the sailors chased us back down. We had to stay belowdecks until everyone was aboard. I began to worry about the men dehydrating and possible heatstroke. This was my third voyage on a troop ship, and I figured we would start getting some air when we got under way.

No such luck.

That night we tried to sleep up on deck. My section carved out a space near the stern. The wind whipped around the deck and felt good after being in the bowels of the ship for so long. When the captain saw all of us on deck, he ordered the crew to chase us back down to our troop compartment. Sleeping on the deck was too dangerous, the captain said. A rogue wave could sweep us overboard or we could get fouled up on the equipment on the deck.

The trip was hot and boring. We got two meals a day, which was normal for a troop ship. Because the ship was so crowded, by the time everybody got breakfast it was almost noontime, so the galley immediately started to work on dinner. The old joke was to hurry up and eat so you could get back in line for the next meal.

Standing on deck one night after chow, I stared out into the dark Pacific. I was leaning on the rail, drifting into my own little world. The girl from Vallejo's questions had me thinking. Since I'd become section leader, my goal was to make sure my men were ready. But was I? It wouldn't be long and I would be facing the test of my life. I was staring down at the water thinking about fear. Yes, I was scared, I was really scared that I might not be able to provide my men the leadership they deserved once we got into combat.

My thoughts wandered to my first voyage.

I'd left New Jersey in 1946 heading for Italy. Sailing through the Strait of Gibraltar into the Mediterranean Sea, I could see the Rock of Gibraltar in the distance. It was exciting; however, I was apprehensive not knowing what I had to face. I'd never been this far from home.

We docked in Naples and drove cross-country in a truck. Seeing the devastation of Cassino shocked me. The entire town was nothing but rubble. This was my first real look at war. It's one thing to see it in photos but shocking to see it in person.

Late in the afternoon we arrived in Foggia on the Adriatic

side of Italy. We drove up to a bombed out factory where three hundred German prisoners were being held in winterized tents. Most of them had been captured in North Africa and belonged to one company. We joined an Italian Army company just outside of the factory area. The Italians and the Americans combined to provide security for the area.

That first night I was taken out to one of the warehouses and put on a guard post. Supposedly, there was an Italian guard on the post with me, but I didn't see him anywhere. I was in the dark, didn't know where I was, and didn't know where the Italian was. I began to see something in every shadow and over the chattering of my teeth heard unexplained noises in every direction. All of a sudden I heard the crunching of gravel and someone came out of the darkness. My hand shook from fear as much as the cold.

"Halt," I shouted.

The shadow said something in Italian and kept coming.

"Fraido? Fraido?" he said.

I figured the son of a bitch was asking me if I was afraid. I shook my head no. He smiled, turned around and walked off back into the darkness. I watched him leave and walk toward some fires. I shifted from foot to foot trying to stay warm. All of a sudden out of the shadows came my Italian partner, walking along as calmly as when he left. He handed me his canteen cup and it was full of coffee. He gestured to me to drink.

The next morning I went to the old factory washroom.

When I went to the sink to wash my hands, I noticed that the faucets were labeled *caldo* and *fraido*. *Caldo* was warm and *fraido* was cold. The guy last night was asking me if I was cold.

I realized that fear comes from the unknown, and the unknown was never as bad as I initially thought. Overcoming fear needed to become second nature.

After eight days onboard the ship, word spread that we were getting close to Japan. We'd do another month of training before landing in Korea. We crowded along the rail looking at the shore lights in the distance. The water made the lights from the city look like stars.

"It's Yokohama and we're headed right for it," I heard a soldier say.

Suddenly the ship started slowly turning to the starboard and running south, parallel to the shore. I didn't think much of it. But the next morning we were informed that we were going straight to Korea.

CHAPTER FOUR

PUSAN

The smell was unbearable.

The water around the dock at Pusan was black and slick with oil and sewage. Two docks up from where we were was a cattle holding area, and when they cleaned the pens they just hosed everything into the water.

The pungent odor hit us as we approached the pier. Most of the guys stayed below, out of the smell, but I stayed on the deck mesmerized by the port.

Tucked into the southeastern tip of the Korean Peninsula, Pusan was Korea's largest port. Thousands of U.N. soldiers were moving through this port. Everywhere you looked there were cranes, trucks and trains, all in constant motion. The piers were clogged with green Army trucks and crates of ammunition and food. Cranes lifted the supplies to the dock and forklifts zigzagged around bringing them to waiting trains. It was a complex, modern ballet of engines and men, and we'd arrived right in the middle of it. The docks and railroads reminded me of Philadelphia.

Before we got off the ship, I pulled my section aside.

"A lot of you men have never seen a harbor. This one is busy and dangerous. Keep your heads up and make sure you stay out of the way of the cranes."

The men nodded and we marched down the ramp to the dock. My company was quartered in a huge shed right on the dock. Winn told us that we'd be there a few days, until the ship was downloaded. The shed was dark and we were given a small spot to sleep. We used our shelter halves and blankets and slept on the floor. The grumbling started almost immediately.

Walsh took his shelter half and laid it close to me. "What a shit hole," he said. That about summed up everybody's attitude. And after two hot meals a day on the ship, we were now stuck eating C rations.

One daily ration had six twelve-ounce cans. Three of either meat and beans, meat and potato hash, or meat and vegetable stew, and three bread and dessert cans with crackers. We used a key, soldered to the bottom of one can, to open the rest of the three-and-a-half-inch-tall tinplate cans. The ration also came with a packet of gum, toilet paper, matches and a nine-pack of cigarettes. Everyone carried an opener on his dog tag chain.

During the first night, Vaillancourt came to me and asked if I could give a couple of thirty-round magazines to an old friend of his. On the trip over, I'd scrounged the magazines from the anti-aircraft unit to replace the fifteen-round magazines we had been issued. I then had my guys tape the bigger magazines together so that all they had to do was flip them to reload.

"Sure," I said. "If he is a friend."

"We fought together during the last one," Vaillancourt said.

As we walked down the dock, I could see similar sheds crammed with men. Some stood outside smoking. Others just stood outside trying to get a little fresh air. After a few hours, the smell didn't really bother us anymore. Now, it was just the waiting.

The lieutenant was sitting on his cot writing a letter. He smiled when Vaillancourt came in.

"This is Corporal Richardson, sir. He has a few magazines for you."

The lieutenant smiled and we shook hands. I handed him about a half dozen magazines. "This is all I can spare, sir."

"Thanks, Corporal."

"Hey, sir," I said. "What are you hearing?"

The lieutenant shook his head.

The American Eighth Army had established a perimeter to hold off the Korean People's Army until enough troops could arrive and organize a counteroffensive. Set up in August, the perimeter's western boundary was formed mostly by the Nak-tong River, and the Sea of Japan formed the eastern boundary. The northern boundary followed a jagged line of mountains north of the city.

"The North Koreans crossed the Naktong River today. I'm not sure how that looks on the map, I really haven't seen one yet."

I looked at Vaillancourt and then back at the lieutenant.

"I know one thing," I said. "If you're defending a river and the enemy is on your side, you're in trouble."

"Maybe it won't be that bad when we get there," Vaillan-court said.

We got our chance to see a few days later. At first, the men seemed happy to finally be moving, but soon it sank in that in a day or two we'd be in combat. We started breaking down our gear. I was determined to keep everybody busy, including myself.

That evening, after another dinner of C rations, I got the section together.

"I want everybody to check his gear one more time. We're moving to an assembly area north of Taegu first thing in the morning," I said. "And take a moment and write home. You never know when you'll get another chance."

I dismissed them and hustled off to another meeting. On top of getting my own gear ready, I had to make sure our equip-ment was ready to move north. I got busy and failed to follow my own advice. I'd gotten as far as finding paper and envelopes, but never put pen to paper. That night, I thought of my dad and his new life. And I thought of my mother and Frank, but most of all I thought of my brothers and sisters. I hoped they weren't worrying too much.

The next morning, before we loaded on the trains, the word was put out to leave our duffel bags. They'd catch up with us later.

"Get your personal items out of your bags and anything else you want," I said. "Make sure you have three or four pairs of socks. And if you aren't sure, leave it. Your whole life is about to become what's in your combat pack and bedroll."

I had a tailor-made uniform in my duffel bag and I knew I could kiss it good-bye. I grabbed my socks, some additional pairs of underwear and a small can of foot powder.

Sitting on my now useless duffel bag, I waited for the order to board the train. My thoughts strayed to a bombed out railroad platform in Castle, Germany. As in the rest of the city, there was very little left standing. Wherever there was a partial wall, it was plastered with notes from people trying to find their loved ones.

A train load of German prisoners of war was returning from the Soviet Union. A small knot of civilians waited for the soldiers to get off the train, hoping that one could be their father, husband or brother.

Seeing them in dirty and threadbare uniforms that hung on their bony frames, I couldn't imagine how much weight they'd lost. Or understand the misery they'd suffered. As they passed me, I saw nothing in their dark, dead eyes. It was as if they'd died already and their bodies were on autopilot. This was not the way to come home from war.

Then, suddenly, a young woman, not more than twenty-one years old, bolted from the group of civilians on the platform. I watched her sundress flap behind her as she weaved through the column of former prisoners.

"Daddy, Daddy."

She had spotted her father and run to him. He looked down and the faraway gaze melted off his face. His eyes came alive and he reached out and hugged her. They both started sobbing and holding each other. I turned away and saw the rest of the civilians turn away and leave the platform. Only a few stayed to watch. One older woman just stood on the platform and stared, tears running down her worn cheeks.

The trains to Taegu left just after noon. I heard a few cheers as the train picked up momentum. The train lumbered down the track for a while then stopped at a siding. Word came back that we were near the assembly area, but had to make way for a hospital train headed south. The train carrying the wounded stopped for a few moments and we could see the soldiers inside. IV bags hung next to litters. Men with bandaged arms, legs and heads lined the cars. The few walking wounded stared out the windows. Like the German prisoners, the wounded Americans had dark, depressing eyes and a vacant stare. A few of our guys tried to pass them cigarettes and candy from the window, but they didn't react. They just stared into space.

"God, I wish they'd move us," I said to Walsh.

"Rich, you think they came from where we're going?"

Heaggley and some of the others heard us and turned to me.

I was thinking the same thoughts.

"I don't think so," I said, turning from the sad scene.

The assembly area was full of soldiers and equipment headed toward the front. We were assigned the mission as regimental reserve. The next morning, we got orders to move forward. The North Koreans had penetrated some defense positions along the main road to Taegu, the South Korean's temporary capital. We were to move north along the main road and retake the lost ground.

I gathered up my section in a semicircle and started to explain the mission. Everybody seemed edgy. Nervous talk or dead silence. Not much in between. Taking my helmet off, I had knelt down when I heard the crack of a rifle and felt a bullet race past my head. I signaled the section to remain seated, stood up and started looking around.

"Where the hell did that come from?" I said, scanning the faces of the men.

I looked back to see my section staring back at me, stunned. In the back, I saw Heaggley lean over and whisper to Walsh.

"He never flinched," he said. "He just went on talking."

I knelt down again and kept talking. If they saw it that way, better for me.

"Okay, goddamn it. You all couldn't have a better lesson than what just happened," I said in a growl. "From now on, weapons will be loaded with safeties on. This must become second nature to everyone. Do you understand?"

After my speech, we got on the trucks and headed toward the front. Someone slammed a Browning automatic rifle butt on the bed of one of the other trucks and three or four rounds went off, arcing high into the sky above us. I flinched this time. My nerves were fried. Despite what my section thought, after that first shot I'd almost shit my pants.

CHAPTER FIVE

BAPTISM OF FIRE

As the trucks rumbled forward, we could see American troops moving south down the road. They looked like ghosts, frail, with torn and dirty uniforms. Their black eyes didn't even register as we passed. They had the infantryman's thousand-yard stare. They were lost. Gone.

The trucks pulled off the road and we jumped off the back. There was a sense of urgency as we got organized and started moving toward the village of Tabu-Dong on the horizon. Tabu-Dong sat astride a fork in the road, dubbed the bowling alley because the constant rumble of artillery up and down the valley sounded like pins falling.

We were operating under Lieutenant General Walton H. Walker's standing order to "stand or die." Walker, the Eighth

Army commander, had issued the order in July, before we'd arrived.

"We are fighting a battle against time. There will be no more retreating, withdrawal or readjustment of the lines or any other term you choose. There is no line behind us to which we can retreat. . . . There will be no Dunkirk, there will be no Bataan. A retreat to Pusan would be one of the greatest butcheries in history. We must fight until the end. . . . We will fight as a team. If some of us must die, we will die fighting together. . . . I want everybody to understand we are going to hold this line. We are going to win."

Thick black smoke rose in a steady stream on the other side of the horizon. I could see only a few of the squat huts, but the valley and ridges had thick scraggly bushes, which made it very difficult to see any movement.

Suddenly artillery shells and mortar rounds crashed down around us. We dove into the ditches that lined the road and waited for the barrage to end. I waved to my section and got them together before we moved out toward the outskirts of the village. A smoky haze with the pungent smell of gunpowder hung over us as we started moving forward. I could feel my heart beating and my breaths came quickly, almost like I was running. But it wasn't nerves. It was adrenaline. My body was on fire, popping with energy.

Back on the road, a North Korean machine gun to our right opened fire. I could see the tracer rounds in almost slow motion slashing into the line of men ahead of me. The soldiers ducked and dove out of the way as the rounds bit into the dirt around them.

Time is a strange thing in combat. Sometimes it moves so fast that you cannot believe it, and other times it is moving so slowly that you could scream. We dove into the dirt and pressed ourselves flat against the ground. McAbee started moving the other platoons toward the guns while my section, part of the weapons platoon, provided supporting fire.

This was real combat. All of my fears seemed so far away now. I didn't have time to worry about how I'd react. I just had to act. Turning back toward Walsh's gun, I yelled for him to get in position and start firing at the machine guns.

Walsh nodded and started calling to his men. Like veterans, they ignored the machine gun fire and got the gun up and ready.

"Put some fire on that hill," I shouted, pointing toward the North Korean gunners with my hand.

Walsh pointed out the machine gun position, and Gomez, the assistant gunner, loaded a round and Hall sighted in the gun and fired. My section fired its first shot of the war. The round hit near the gun, and it paused before continuing to fire. By then, Gray had his gun up and both Heaggley and Hall pounded away at the North Korean troops dug in on the hill overlooking the village.

In a matter of minutes, we'd knocked out one of the

machine guns. There was still one more somewhere. I didn't wait for an order and moved both guns up the hill with the lead platoon.

Winn got Vaillancourt, Roberts and me together and told us K Company and I Company were on our left flank. There was an engineer company fighting as infantry located to our left rear, close to the village of Tabu-Dong. Winn placed the mortar section to the left of our position and fifty yards down the reverse slope. He placed me on the right flank of the company.

"Lieutenant, we can bring fire on the North Koreans as they approach, but we won't be much use at night because we won't see them until they get close," I said.

The hill dropped away at such a sharp degree that the 57s would shoot harmlessly over their heads.

"At night we'll just be another rifle platoon, so I'm going to need grenades," I said.

My men didn't have any grenades, but I was happy that I had gotten thirty-round clips from the air defense unit on the ship.

Winn looked at Vaillancourt.

"I got it, Rich," the platoon sergeant said. After the meeting, he pulled me aside.

"We're only getting one C ration per two men."

I shook my head. "That means a meal and a half a day. Supplies are that short? You'll at least have grenades."

"The Army wasn't ready for Korea," Vaillancourt said. "Send a runner back for the grenades."

When I got back to my section, the guys were digging in. I told them to set up the guns, but we'd be covering our section with rifles that night. We were all wired after our first firefight, and it was good that we had something to do. I was happy to see that everybody was digging with a sense of urgency.

I was worried about our open right flank. I ordered the section to dig some positions facing to the right in case we had to occupy them.

When we were done, I told my guys to eat and rest while I got with Walsh and Gray.

"Word is the North Koreans are attacking at night. Take the C ration cans and fill them with rocks," I said. "And tie them at knee height in the bushes in front and to the right of us."

I dug my hole slightly to the rear and in the center of both squads.

"If you need to get to me, come from the side. No one should get out of his position unless it is absolutely necessary. If they get through, stay in your hole because I'm going to shoot anyone standing up."

The men nodded.

"The password tonight is 'north,'" I said. "Response is 'rebel.'"

I had two men in each foxhole. Walsh was with me. I told

Walsh to gather up some small rocks and put them in the bottom of the foxhole. He looked at me like I was crazy.

"What the hell is this for?" he asked.

"We're going to take turns throwing them at any hole that does not answer when we call them. I'm not taking any chances on anyone falling asleep."

That night everyone was on edge. Walsh and I tried to make small talk, but this was not a small talk night. None of us could sleep. Mostly, I called out to my men and scanned the now pitch-black valley. Every noise, smell and shadow drew my interest.

The attack started with a guttural scream. The North Koreans came out of the brush in waves. We could see them moving toward us like shadows. Muzzle flashes exploded out of the darkness. There was very little aimed fire. Instead we were firing straight ahead in their assigned zone. Soon, screams from our wounded joined the chorus of battle cries, orders and machine guns.

Illuminating rounds from our mortar section soon lit up the area like a ballpark, making the North Korean soldiers look like silhouettes on a firing range. We dropped several before the flare burned out. Since the rounds were in short supply, the mortars waited several minutes between rounds.

During a lull, I could hear one of the engineers to our left screaming in pain and calling for his mother. His sobs and screams for help landed harder than the North Korean artillery shells.

Finally, Private Jones, one of my young smart-asses, had heard enough. He started to yell and scream. I covered Walsh as he scrambled out to Jones. He was on the bottom of Hall's hole crying. Walsh tried to get him up, but he wouldn't move. I climbed out and helped Walsh drag Jones's ass out of the foxhole.

"You stay with Hall," I told Walsh.

Snatching Jones by his shirt collar, I stumbled with him back to my foxhole. He crawled in and huddled against the wall sobbing. He couldn't talk, even when I asked him simple questions. His body heaved with every sob.

The engineer had finally stopped screaming and now in an ever desperate voice pleaded for someone to come get him.

"Stay in your holes," I barked.

I was sure the North Koreans were lying in wait hoping someone would try to get him. God, I wished he would die. That thought sent a jolt through me. Jesus Christ, I didn't really mean that. The poor son of a bitch. My only thought now was please God bring the daylight soon.

When the sun's rays finally peeked over the horizon, we started getting the wounded off the hill. The rifle platoon to our left had some men who had been caught sleeping and the Koreans had slit their throats. The section watched as the wounded men walked past with their throats covered in blood, assisted by two men. It was a demoralizing sight—my men were scared shitless—because it could have been us. That would keep them alert at night, I hoped. When the wounded had all been evacuated, I got the medic to tag Jones.

I pulled the medic aside.

"Doc, can you write this up and make sure he never gets sent back?"

"Roger, Sergeant," the medic said, taking Jones by the arm and leading him back to the makeshift casualty collection point on the backside of the hill.

Walsh grabbed me after Jones left. We were getting ready to move forward, and I was making sure Jones hadn't left anything behind.

"Sarge, Black lost it. He's crying and he's hugging a tree and will not respond to me."

Black, I didn't know him very well. He was one of the company's problem children. He'd gotten drunk after a unit picnic at Fort Devens and the military police had locked him up for bring drunk and disorderly. This incident confirmed what I already thought: Black was going to be a constant problem. I put him in Walsh's squad and we'd both kept on his ass making sure he was doing the right thing.

When I got to Black, he was wrapped around a tree like a vine. Every time a shell landed nearby, he began shaking and crying. No talking was going to help. I just wanted to get him away from the rest of the men. The section had fought well, but after listening to the engineer all night they had their own nerves to contend with.

They didn't need to be exposed to this.

"Move the section up the road a little ways while I get a medic to tag him and get him out of here," I told Walsh.

I got the same medic who tagged Jones. That made two men within twenty-four hours. If this continued, I would lose the whole section to fear instead of the enemy.

Greenlowe, my other young guy was doing great as my runner. Last night I sent him back to the company headquarters to pick up the grenades. He assured me that he could find the headquarters location in the dark. Over the next few days he proved his worth so much so that the company commander recognized his courage and ability to find his way around the battlefield and made him the company runner to battalion.

CHAPTER SIX

DARK DAYS OF SUMMER

The heat and humidity covered us like a blanket as we moved north through the village of Tabu-Dong.

In minutes, our fatigues were soaking wet from sweat. We marched for five miles, and with every step I hoped that we didn't get attacked. Moving through the skeleton of houses burned out by constant fighting was eerie. We could see debris and torn clothes in the rubble. I scanned each mud hut as we passed and waited for the ambush around every corner, but the village was deserted and we made it without firing a shot.

We all took turns carrying the guns and ammunition. I didn't want to tire out the gunners. Everybody was shuffling along. It reminded me of the march at Camp Stoneman, but this time we weren't hungover.

Just outside of town, the land spread out into untended fields and rice paddies with the high ridges that formed the bowling alley on both sides. We were moving at a good clip when all of a sudden we were receiving fire from the high ground to our right front.

"Get that gun in that ditch. Fire at the base of the hill," I yelled to Gray. "Walsh, follow me."

We ran into a field where we could get into position to fire

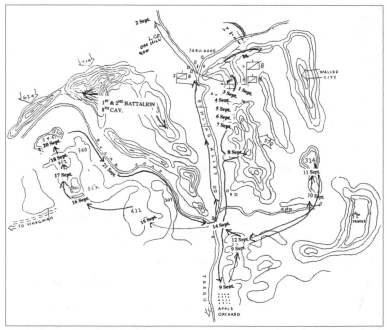

Bowling Alley Pusan perimeter, September 1–23, 1950. Timeline "L" CO & 3rd BN 8th CAV. *National Archives, modified by author.*

at a better angle. It was amazing: Everybody was moving at top speed and just a second ago they were dragging ass.

"Walsh, get in behind that dike, put fire a little further up the hill. Can you see where the fire is coming from?"

"Got it, Rich," Walsh said as his team positioned the gun and started loading.

"I'm going back up the road. Keep your eyes on me," I said. "I'll let you know when I want you."

I caught up with McAbee.

September 6, 1950. Men of 8th CAV., Regt., 1st CAV Division, advance to the front below Tabu-Dong. *National Archives*

65

"Richardson, you keep a machine gun and your 57s firing on the hill. I'm going to attack on the left side. Got it?"

"Yes, sir."

In seconds I could hear Gray's gun start firing and soon after Walsh started pounding the hill. I grabbed Gray and had him fire some white phosphorous—Willie Peter—on the target. The smoke concealed McAbee and the rest of the company as it got into position. I could see our soldiers open fire and start moving up the hill. I shifted the 57s away from them and continued to pound the North Korean machine gunners. In minutes, McAbee and his men overwhelmed the North Korean defenders.

From my vantage point, it looked like it had been scripted for a movie. It was beautiful to watch the soldiers move so perfectly in concert with our fire. A perfectly executed attack. But it seemed too easy. McAbee seemed to think so too and ordered everybody to hurry up the hill and dig in.

We raced up to a ridge and started to dig. By now, my section had become good at quickly getting the guns up and in position. Then, with our now strong backs, we snapped open our entrenching tools and started digging foxholes.

A foxhole was rectangular shaped and deep enough so that we could stand in it with only our head and shoulders exposed. The hole widened at the bottom so that during artillery fire we could crouch down. If we had time, we also dug sumps so that we could kick enemy grenades into them, possibly saving our lives.

At dark, North Korean shells started to crash down around us. Volley after volley showered us with debris. The ground shook like an earthquake, and the roar of the explosions made it impossible to hear or even think.

As I crouched down in my hole, holding my helmet tight against my head, my leg started to shake. I tried to press down on it, but the leg continued to shake and jump. I never got the shakes in the daylight no matter how tough the situation was. Why? I didn't know. Maybe because I could see what was happening around me, I felt more like I was in control. At night it was the unknown that shook me, but when the fighting started I was under control.

The first time this happened to me was when I was fourteen years old. I was being questioned in regards to a payroll robbery of a local company. I had nothing to do with it, but the police still took me in for questioning. During the questioning, my right leg jumped uncontrollably. I stood up to try to stop it but to no avail. I have no idea why my leg shook so badly, because I really was innocent.

I prayed that none of my men ever noticed my leg shaking. Adrenaline always seemed to flow at the right time for me; it was the same playing football: The more often or the harder I got hit, the better I seemed to play.

The smoke and dust still hung in the air when they attacked again. The first waves came with rifles; behind them more soldiers followed and picked up the weapons left by the dead. On almost every attack, the North Koreans tried to slip behind our lines and cut off our avenue of retreat. Once they did, they would pound our flanks. This time, the North Korean soldiers charged up the hill right into the teeth of our machine guns. After the third attempt, they quit and we settled in for a tense night.

We waited all night, but they didn't attack again. The North Koreans instead went around us and cut off the road back to Tabu-Dong. As the fingers of pink light shot up over the horizon, we were ordered to withdraw through the North Korean line. This was not going to be easy.

Just as we were ready to start our dangerous trek, we were notified that the remainder of the battalion had breached the North Korean line close to Tabu-Dong. Colonel Johnson ordered McAbee to withdraw off the ridge. He was sending trucks through the breach in an audacious attempt to get us out.

We found a field near the road where the trucks could turn around, and we dug in. We were in a bad spot and knew it. If the trucks got stopped, there was little hope that we could fight our way back to our lines. If we stayed put, they would smash us with another artillery barrage. And I was sure we wouldn't escape without losses.

I gathered up the section before the trucks arrived.

"Move quickly when the trucks get here. Be prepared to fire as we go down the road. I want everybody facing out," I said as calmly as I could. "I want half of you on each side of the truck ready to fire. Fire on my orders. Look for orange panels. Those are friendlies."

Soon, I could see the trucks coming down the road. Five two-and-a-half-ton trucks. They had machine gun mounts, but since the Army was short, no machine guns. They raced down the road at a breakneck pace. Their engines screamed as the drivers pushed them. They pulled into the field in a semicircle and barely stopped before we started climbing aboard. Things were tight, and in minutes the whole company was crammed into the truck beds. Witt, one of the section's pudgy ammo bearers, tapped me on the shoulder just as the driver started back toward the road.

"Sarge, can I please get on the floor of the truck and pray for us?"

"Okay," I barked. "But you better make it a goddamn good prayer."

The trucks quickly got up to speed. I kept talking and re-peating orders to scan the road and be ready to shoot. Standing near the cab, I watched the truck in front of me swerve and almost lose control. Shit. If one of these trucks crashed, there wasn't enough room to go around it.

Then I saw the panels in the distance. We were getting close to the North Korean line.

I ordered the section to fire. I wanted to keep the North Koreans' heads down. We kept up a steady stream of fire. I have no idea if we hit anything, but I could hear the North Korean rounds hitting our truck. When I saw the panels getting closer, I started shouting to my men.

"Cease fire. Cease fire."

I could hear the fire slack off as each truck passed through. I finally exhaled and watched as the men relaxed. I helped Witt up from the bed of the truck and slapped him on the back.

"Good work," I said. "He listened."

It didn't take long and we were off the trucks and quickly organized to move against a position to the east of the road. This seemed a little crazy. We'd attacked way out in front of our lines and luckily withdrawn through Tabu-Dong; now we were attacking a hill that seemed to be in the rear of the positions we had just passed through.

We were part of Lieutenant General Walton H. Walker's "mobile defense." The strategy focused on using a small number of soldiers to form a thin screen while the bulk of the force waited to counterattack. The idea was unheard of in the 1950s and considered a "theory" at best, but Walker used it to perfection. We could move at ease since the Air Force controlled the skies and there were ample roads and trains so we could flex to trouble areas.

For us ground troops, it was confusing. This game of chess had become maddening. I never had a map and seldom knew the number designation of the hills or objectives. We only knew to move, attack and defend unknown hills that would stop the North Koreans from breaking through and capturing the city of Taegu. This was our world: following orders, fighting for one another, being successful and somehow surviving.

So once we made it back to our side, we quickly moved up another unnamed hill against light resistance. When we got to the top, Vaillancourt contacted me on the radio and told me to go to the reverse side of the hill and wait.

There were a lot of dead North Korean bodies on the hill, most of them bloated from the heat. It looked as if they had been stacked there for a couple of days. While we were waiting for orders, we broke out some C rations, and my mind drifted away to Philadelphia. A neighborhood drunk was passed out on the sidewalk and someone had placed a penny on his nose. The older guys hanging on the street corner were egging the kids on to try to take it off. We were all too scared to try to do it. Finally, I tried, but as I moved close to the drunk he grunted and scared the hell out of me. Now here I was sitting on the ground eating beside stinking dead bodies, and a penny on a drunk's nose didn't seem to be too bad. Life is strange.

Vaillancourt came over from the company command post and woke me out of my daydream.

"Rich, get your men moving. I'll show you where to go. McAbee wants you on the right flank to cover a draw."

I shouted to the men. "Saddle up, we're moving out."

Vaillancourt pointed out a draw to the right side of the ridge. Before he left, I asked about Winn. I hadn't seen the lieutenant for days.

"Is he dead?" I asked.

"No idea, Rich," Vaillancourt said. "He disappeared. Haven't seen him in forty-eight hours."

I never saw Winn again. To this day I have no idea what happened to him.

As we were moving to our position, I touched base with Sergeant Herbert (Pappy) Miller, who was occupying the last position of the First Platoon. Miller was from Pulaski, New York. He'd served in World War II, but after the war he couldn't find a decent job. So he enlisted, and had three months to go before we left for Korea.

"We're tying in with you. We're going to cover the draw on your right flank," I told him.

"Great," Miller said. He and Gray were friends from back at Fort Devens. I heard Miller tell Gray that the platoon had been hit hard on the first day.

The ridge looked familiar to me, and after a few minutes I realized we'd been there before. For a change it was a half-decent position for the 57s. I planned to put one gun on the left side of the draw and the other on the right side. The squads would be separated by twenty yards. I showed Gray where I wanted him to put his squad and told him to come with Walsh and me to the other gun position. I needed to talk to both of them about how we were going to cover the draw that night.

"I'm not feeling very good. I need to sit down for a few minutes," Gray said. His head was pounding and he felt dizzy.

"Try to come over as soon as you can. Are you going to be all right?"

"Yeah, just give me a few minutes."

When we got to the other side of the ridge, I turned and looked back at Gray sitting on a tree stump. He had his head in his hands. Gray and Walsh had been great squad leaders and I hoped he was okay. I needed him and his leadership.

I had taken off my helmet to wipe away some sweat when Gray and the stump suddenly disappeared in a fireball. An artillery round landed right on him. I was stunned and just stood on the ridge looking at the smoking crater.

Something happens to men who see combat. No matter how you try, you cannot make death invisible, it is there with you every moment. That split second would be seared into my mind for the rest of my life. But at the time, we didn't have time to mourn Gray. We had to get dug in.

"Start digging. That round has us zeroed in and the barrage will be coming next," I said, grabbing Walsh.

"Get Hall over to take charge of Gray's squad. Tell him I'll be over to talk to him later."

For the rest of the day I kept the men busy. Anything to keep their minds off Gray. What drove me more than anything was a positive outlook and the fact that my men were watching everything I did. I often wondered when we were moving down the road what went through their minds.

It had to be a lot tougher on them than on me. While they had only death to dwell on, I had dozens of things that I must be thinking about and be prepared for. What was ahead? Where would I be if I were a North Korean? How would I react if we got hit from the right or left? How was our ammunition? Water? Was the bore sighting of the guns still all right? Were the men taking care of their feet?

Luckily, the barrage never came. But I knew that we wouldn't be so lucky when it got dark. Standing in my hole, I took a deep breath. The first attack started soon after the sun set. We could hear them coming up the hill. Artillery rounds slamming into the ground farther down the line rattled off the walls of the valley. I squinted into the darkness looking for the shadows.

The first North Korean assault started with screams and machine gun fire, but we beat it back with mortars and our own machine gun fire. Running between holes, I made sure everybody was ready for the next wave. Walsh had his section up and ready to fire. Hall was also ready, which was impressive since he had just taken over from Gray.

The second attack was worse. The North Korean soldiers were less than fifty yards from us.

As I fired at the shadows moving toward us, I heard a frantic voice come on the radio.

"Roy Rogers 3," the voice said in a deep Southern drawl.

"I needs mo' firepower. I needs mo' firepower. I'm about to get overrun."

It was Lieutenant Jim Brown from the platoon that was on our left. I hoped to hell he got more fire support. We were all hanging by a thread.

Dead North Korean soldiers were stacking up in front of our foxholes. But they kept coming. Wave after wave.

I could hear Walsh screaming at the men to stay in their holes. I was frantically changing the magazine in my carbine as two of the North Koreans were within ten feet of me. Walsh and Hall saw them too and opened fire, cutting the North Korean soldiers down. I saw another North Korean to my right and fired. He staggered back and dropped to the ground.

I stayed low in my foxhole and kept firing straight ahead. Hall and Walsh kept firing to the rear, hitting the North Koreans attempting to move through our position. We had them in a cross fire, and in minutes our position was littered with North Korean bodies. Sliding a fresh magazine into my carbine, I poked my head up waiting for the next wave. But it never came.

"Stay alert. Some of them may be alive. If you see any movement, shoot them."

We waited a few minutes and then finally climbed out.

"Check around your holes for live Koreans."

The bodies of about a half dozen North Korean soldiers lay crumpled in between our foxholes. I slowly picked my way, my rifle at the ready. My nerves were on fire. I'd never been this close and was ready for even a slight movement. Two were badly wounded and kept muttering in Korean. I saw Hall kick their weapons away and then drag them to the rear of our position. Eventually our medics would take care of them. We dragged the rest of the bodies away from our position and piled them to one side. I didn't look at their faces. I didn't care.

As daylight peeked its head over the hills, a tall, scrubby-looking infantryman carrying a carbine approached me from out of the mist. As he got closer, I saw the small white cross painted on his helmet. He stuck out his hand as he approached.

"Chaplain Kapaun," he said, giving me a firm handshake. "Where are you from?"

Chaplain Emil Kapaun, from Pilsen, Kansas, was a Catholic father who joined the Army toward the end of World War II. He served in Burma and India until May 1946. He returned home and was assigned a parish in Kansas. But he felt his calling was with the troops, so rejoined the Army in 1948. He joined us in Korea after spending a few months in Japan.

His uniform was dirty and he, like the rest of us, needed a shave. It was clear he'd spent the night close to the fighting and not safely in the rear. There was a peacefulness about him, though, that put me at ease. A quiet confidence. He seemed to care where I was from, and I watched him as he spoke to the rest of the section. Each time, he asked where the soldier was from and gave him a firm handshake. It was not long before he had us all smiling.

When Kapaun finished making his rounds, he sat down near my foxhole and took out his pipe. It was missing most of its stem.

"What happened to your pipe?" I asked, as he filled it.

"A sniper," he said. "Shot it out of my mouth a few days ago."

We both had a laugh. I noticed the carbine lying across his lap.

"I thought chaplains couldn't carry weapons."

He smiled and nodded. "If they are going to shoot at me I'm going to be ready to shoot back."

With that, he stood up and, cradling his wounded pipe, disappeared over the ridge to visit Miller's men.

For the next five days we found ourselves fighting south and east of the road junction at Tabu-Dong. We attacked during the day and defended against their attacks at night. Due to casualties in the battalion, the three rifle companies were beginning to look like three rifle platoons. My section was down to eight men.

We received two replacements. They showed up with their gear and clean uniforms. One was named Jackson, but I didn't catch the other's name. Jackson had a lot of questions about the North Koreans and where we were on the line. I tried to answer what I could but was content to let Hall and Walsh deal with him. I just gave both of the new men a little advice.

"Stay close to your foxhole partner and listen to him," I said. "We have a very fluid situation, so act quickly and do what you are told."

I didn't see them until the next morning. We'd been attacked again, but this time we were able to keep the North Koreans from our lines. But not without cost. Three men were gone; one missing and two wounded, including both replacements. The missing one, Jackson, had just gotten up and left. Walsh said Jackson's brother had been missing in action since July and he volunteered to come to Korea so he could find him. After the attack, he climbed out of his foxhole and walked into the darkness. We never saw him again.

We were taking casualties every night and soon could no longer hold our position south of Tabu-Dong. The constant North Korean attacks drove us south to the lower slopes of Hill 570. It had been raining constantly for two days as we dug into yet another new position on the slope; later that night we got orders to withdraw. Withdrawing in the daylight was bad enough. Now we were going to attempt it at night. I led Hall's squad out first since they'd lost two men in an attack that afternoon. When I got back for Walsh, everybody was ready to go. I ordered everybody to move out. Walsh took the lead while I waited for the last men to go. Everyone got up with the exception of one man. He was lying on the ground under his poncho. I pushed him with my boot.

"Let's go," I whispered. I was nervous and wanted to get going before another attack.

Walsh, standing nearby, looked over at me.

"Sarge, that's Johnson. He's dead."

I felt terrible. It hurt to see another one of my men dead in the mud. I didn't even know Johnson that well. He was another replacement and I'd only just learned his name. The fact that I had little time to dwell saved me. Plus, I knew that if I showed weakness my men might finally give in and feel sorry for themselves, and I couldn't have that. We needed to stick together. I became stoic and would remain that way for a long time.

Grabbing two of his unit mates, it was so dark I wasn't sure who, I told them to pick Johnson up and carry him out of there. We started to head toward the assembly point on the other side of the hill. Once we were on the road, the movement was agonizingly slow. We moved for about an hour and then stopped. I was called to the front of the column with all of the platoon leaders.

It was another attack.

"The entire battalion is going to attack Hill 570. Three ridges go direct to the top of the hill. K Company will be on the left, we will move in the center, and I Company on the right," McAbee said. "We will attack at daylight with no artillery or air support. The Second and Third platoons will attack abreast,

Second on the right, Third on the left. Richardson will follow with 57s in the center; the First Platoon will be in reserve."

The hill, two miles southwest of the village of Ka-san, was a strategic point because it overlooked the Taegu Road. The hill was defended by bunkers, and intelligence reports said the North Koreans would likely make a strong stand there because once it fell, the way would be open for unrestricted advance.

A thick fog hugged the ground as we climbed Hill 570. We knew the North Koreans were on the top of the ridge waiting. The climb was steep and took us a while. I knew the North Koreans were just waiting for us to get into range. When we were halfway up, they finally opened up on us with machine guns and mortars.

I kept my head down and kept climbing. There was nothing else to do. I didn't think about getting killed. I only worried about my men. I constantly urged them to keep climbing. We couldn't stop. And we didn't.

Soon, the firing stopped, the North Koreans withdrawing farther up the hill. The visibility was getting better as we kept moving up. Still we had not made contact with the main Korean positions.

All of a sudden we started receiving fire from the positions on the top of the hill. I could see men from the other platoons running from the machine gun and mortar fire. Many of them were being hit by shrapnel from the mortar fire. We were panicking.

"Stay down," I yelled at my men as soldiers from the other platoons brushed by us heading down. If they tried to run, they would be cut down by the mortar fire.

Climbing behind a cluster of rocks, I managed to hold my men in place. But there was no one in front of us. Since they didn't have any targets, the North Koreans slacked off in their firing. I knew we couldn't take the hill alone. I kept the men in position, and shortly after, Lieutenant Peterson, the company executive officer, came up the hill.

"How many men do you have?" he asked.

"I've got two 57s and all my men."

"Move up the hill a little more and hold the position until I get back," he said.

I just looked at him. He looked me straight in the eye. "Got it?"

"Yes, sir."

He turned around and went back down the hill. I realized that I'd never told him how many men I had. I was sitting there with only eight men counting myself.

I moved up the hill until we started receiving fire. I had my men spread across a finger of high ground. I stayed in the center. We set up behind rocks and holes dug from artillery rounds. We were lying there no more than thirty or forty yards from the North Koreans and nobody was behind us. Every once in a while we would receive sporadic small arms fire.

"Hey, Sarge, how long are we going to be here?" Walsh first.

"Sarge, we're getting out of here by dark, right?" Hall second.

I knew the other men wouldn't speak up, but I could look in their eyes and see they were scared. I just hoped they couldn't see the fear in my eyes.

"We're staying until we get orders," I said, finally answering Walsh and Hall.

I spoke up loud enough for the whole section to hear. Farther down the hill, mortar and artillery fire was very heavy. We could see the North Korean positions and they could see us. I was hoping we were out of grenade range and too close to their position for them to put mortar fire on us. Soon, instead of mortars, the North Korean soldiers started sending down taunts. We didn't speak the language, but each word had a charge.

"Silence. No one talks back," I whispered and put my finger to my lips. Not that we knew what they were saying.

As the minutes and then hours ticked off, I realized that slowly but surely we were moving back a foot at a time. A guy would reposition and then the rest of the section would go off of him. At this rate, we might be off the hill by the end of the war. I knew one thing, there was no way we were staying overnight.

I didn't know how long we were there, but finally I heard someone coming. It was Vaillancourt. He signaled me to withdraw. I told Walsh and Hall to fire one 57 round each on my order and for everyone to immediately start moving down the hill. Everyone got ready.

I raised my hand, dropped it and shouted, "Fire!"

They fired simultaneously, and immediately we started running down the hill. What seemed like only a few seconds later we started receiving small arms fire. I was hoping all the way that we wouldn't receive any mortar fire.

"Where's the executive officer?" I asked Vaillancourt when I caught up with him.

"He was killed along with one of the platoon leaders. The company had regrouped and tried to come back up the hill but was ripped apart by heavy mortar and artillery fire. We lost the two lieutenants and two platoons took heavy losses."

"How did you know we were still up there?"

"Lieutenant Brown and the first platoon were moving into position to continue the attack when the battalion commander issued the order to withdraw. That's when Captain McAbee told me you were on the hill and for me to get you down."

Back on the road, we started to take mortar fire from the hill. The road had deep culverts that ran from one side to the other. The ditches were big enough for a man to go through standing up. I quickly ushered my men down into one of them. We got three quarters of the way through the culvert and ran into two dead North Koreans and an American soldier. The Koreans were lying in a heap, and the soldier, a lieutenant, was holding his head and moaning in pain. When I got there, Vaillancourt had him by his collar and was dragging him to the other end of the culvert.

The lieutenant was Vaillancourt's friend from Pusan, the one that needed the large magazines. We drug him out of the culvert and got a medic to take care of him. I found out years later that he'd been withdrawing down the culvert when he stumbled into the North Koreans. Luckily, he'd been able to get two shots off, but they had too. One North Korean bullet struck him in the chest, but a near fatal shot was deflected by the magazine. He was lucky.

As we got farther down the road, men from the battalion sat along both sides of the road. None of the companies had succeeded in securing their objective. We were a sad-looking bunch as we moved to what looked like an orchard. We were told we were going to stay there awhile to rest and reorganize.

I pulled my now eight-man section off to one side of the orchard. We threw our packs to the ground and sprawled out dead tired. The men were in good spirits, and before the first bite of my C ration they were trading barbs.

Hall started in on his typical complaint.

"If I never dig another foxhole again that will be too soon," he said between bites of pork and beans. "By now I could have tunneled to China."

"We should write Sears and Roebuck for an automatic foxhole digger," I said. "They have everything else."

Everybody started to laugh.

"Great idea, Sarge," Hall said.

"Tear a cover off a C ration box," I said.

"What for, Sarge?"

"I'm going to write a letter to Sears on it."

"You're shitting us," Hall said.

"Nope. I'm not," I said as I started writing and addressing it to Sears on Roosevelt Boulevard in Philadelphia.

"It will never get there," Walsh said.

"If it gets back to the APO, they will send it," I said, signing my name.

They all laughed.

While we were talking, McAbee came up with Colonel Johnson. He motioned for me to join them.

I put my letter aside and ran over to him.

"Sergeant Richardson and his men were the last ones off the hill," McAbee told Colonel Johnson.

"How are your men doing?" the colonel asked, looking over my shoulder at the men finishing up the letter to Sears.

"Okay, but they're very tired."

Johnson nodded and shook my hand. "Try and get some rest tonight."

He started to walk away. Frustrated with the attack, I knew this was my chance to speak my mind and the mind of my men. I wanted to know how many more times we were going to have to climb up a hill only to leave it and fight our way up another. From my point of view, we were just getting our asses kicked.

"How are we doing? It seemed like we never make any headway."

Johnson stopped.

"Sergeant Richardson, you tell your men they did a great job. Against great odds we have stopped the North Koreans' main attack."

I turned away and slowly walked back toward the men. I thought to myself how great Walsh, Hall and Heaggley were. It was their courage and bravery that held us together. As I looked at them it almost brought tears to my eyes.

CHAPTER SEVEN

TIDE TURNS

Johnson's news had an immediate impact on my section.

We no longer dragged ass. Instead, we seemed hopeful. Optimistic even. Before dark our company was ordered to occupy the high ground north of the apple orchard. So much for a rest. We barely got to the high ground and it started to get dark. The position was a short distance from the south end of the ridge we'd failed to take—Hill 570. Obviously we were in a blocking position in case the North Koreans continued to attack south during the night.

For the next two days, we attacked to the east and took Hill 314. On the final day, K Company moved through us and started up the hill. My section was set up and laying down a base of fire. The hill was totally barren, and from my foxhole the attack looked like a demonstration. Like a sand table with an instructor moving toy soldiers toward the objective. There was no movement on the hill. Friendly mortar and artillery fire had lifted. It looked like this was going to be an easy one. K Company had made it almost to the North Korean forward positions when mortar and artillery fire thundered down on them.

"Look on top of the hill," I shouted to Walsh and Hall. "Fire! Fire, on top of the hill."

We could see the North Koreans pouring over the hill. They looked like red ants swarming toward K Company, who were

September 12, 1950. 3rd Battalion advances to road junction.
National Archives

pinned down. Pressing my binoculars to my eyes, I watched the North Koreans pull machine guns into their fighting holes. Soon, their gunners were delivering withering fire on K Company, who was falling back. What moments ago had been a clean, orderly demonstration had erupted into total chaos. The entire forward crest of the hill was a killing zone and K Company was being decimated.

The North Korean artillery fire followed K Company down the hill. The ground shook like an earthquake as the rounds walked toward us. I hugged the bottom and side of the hole. All I could think about was a round landing right on top of me. If it happened, I'd never know. I pulled my helmet and gritted my teeth. I was starting to lose it.

The smoke from the gunpowder was so thick it was beginning to choke me. When is it going to stop? Were they going to follow this up with an attack? Christ, I hoped not. God only knew what the hell we would have left after this. The fire finally lifted and then stopped. I popped my head up and saw men running by our position screaming for us to leave.

I saw Walsh nearby. "Check your men."

I climbed out and went to see how Hall had made out.

"What kind of shape are you in?"

He looked shell-shocked. His face was streaked with dirt and mud. Everybody seemed on edge, but under control.

"We are okay. Only one slightly wounded but he'll be all right."

"Okay. Keep your head down. Tell Heaggley to be ready. The goddamn gooks may try to retake this hill."

"Are we going to stay?"

"Goddamn it, just stay in these holes until I tell you differently."

I raced back to my hole. On the way, a young lieutenant ran by me; he was so scared his voice cracked when he screamed at me.

"Get out of here. Fall back."

"Who the hell are you?" I barked.

There were men still trying to get back, and if we left they wouldn't have a chance in hell.

He didn't stop and I never got his name. He just yelled to fall back.

"You're full of shit," I yelled at him. "We can't leave here. We have to help these men."

Several other members of K Company passed me, following the lieutenant. I saw some of my men getting out of their holes.

"You sons of bitches get back in your goddamn holes," I yelled. "Get back."

They scrambled back. Rounds started to crash around us again. I could hear the K Company men scream as shrapnel showered them, slicing into their skin. Larger pieces punched holes in their chests or sheered off limbs. Their screams filled in the silence between the crashes of artillery shells. I was not going to be able to control this fucking situation much longer.

Walsh just stared at me with a vacant look. Don't lose it now, I thought. Another barrage landed nearby. I put my head down. My ears started ringing. Smoke was down on the bottom of the hole again. The artillery fire finally stopped. The screaming for the medics began.

"Go check your men," I told Walsh, shaking him out of his stupor.

I headed over to Hall's position. He had the same vacant look as Walsh. Men from K Company were moving down the ridge carrying the wounded. Everybody was bleeding or bandaged. I kept my men focused on the hill, waiting for the North Koreans to counterattack. But they never came. Neither did the artillery. It wasn't long and I was told to withdraw off the hill. As I passed the command group, I stepped aside while the section kept moving. I was pissed and let McAbee know about the lieutenant.

"That is the kind of shit that is going to get us all killed," I said, clearly enraged.

"I got it, Richardson. Let it go and I'll take care of it," he told me.

Back at the company assembly area, the men rested on their packs, some dozing, others just staring blankly into space. I took a moment to look at what was left of the company. We'd gotten some replacements, but the company had only sixty-eight men. Five or six had been wounded and returned to the line still bandaged up. One of our machine gunners had been wounded three times and was also back. If this was winning, I didn't want to lose.

While we rested, I noticed a new group of replacements. South Korean conscripts. It was bad enough to come into a unit as a replacement. I couldn't imagine being a Korean and winding up with an American unit.

Vaillancourt brought six South Koreans to me.

"Your new guys," he said.

The South Koreans looked at Vaillancourt. They didn't understand a word and looked scared to death. Dressed in American fatigues, they cradled old M-1 rifles and had small backpacks. They were skinnier than us, but that was changing since we were still on half rations.

I thanked Vaillancourt and smiled at my six new soldiers. They were from the Korean Augmentation to the U.S. Army (KATUSA) program. KATUSA soldiers were young men picked up in the larger cities, given a couple of weeks' training and assigned to American units. Looking over the group, I spotted one that I seemed to connect with. He was stockier than the others and had bright, alert eyes. I tried to talk with him and he just smiled at me. I named him Tony because it sounded similar to his Korean name, and I explained to him that I was calling him that. He shook his head yes and repeated "Tony" and pointed to himself.

I separated them and assigned each small group to my two squads. Tony and the others were mainly used as ammunition bearers. We loaded them up as pack mules and they became an integral part of our firepower.

We lost two of the new Koreans the first day. One was killed and another badly wounded. A couple of days later, I received a replacement for one of them. Tony took charge of him right away. By now, he'd proven to be the most capable and the de facto leader. We had come up with a simple shorthand using English words and hand gestures.

Despite the language barriers, the Koreans fell right in with the rest of us. When we marched, they kept up. When we fought, they stood their ground too. But we found out early on that our C rations were too concentrated for their systems and they just couldn't eat them. The canned meat and beans upset their stomachs. After a lot of trial and error, we finally found that they could handle rice and vegetables. I made sure the section saved those rations for the South Koreans. But as did all soldiers, they liked chocolate.

Not long after Tony arrived, Captain McAbee was promoted to battalion operations officer. He would make a good operations officer because he certainly understood the problems at the company level. Lieutenant Paul Bromser replaced him as company commander. Unlike McAbee, Bromser was quiet and seemed unsure of himself.

Early in the morning the company joined a coordinated attack against Hills 401 and 307. We managed to sweep the North Koreans off the hill, but not without heavy casualties. Early in the attack Lieutenant Brown, the leader of the First Platoon who'd begged for more firepower days earlier, was seriously wounded and taken off the hill on a litter. "Old Firepower Brown" was the last of the platoon leaders who'd left with us from Fort Devens. He would be missed. He was one of the best. There were fewer and fewer soldiers from Fort Devens. Luckily, in my section, I still had Walsh, Hall and Heaggley.

The North Koreans were well entrenched on Hill 312. The mountain was critical terrain because it overlooked the approaches to the Naktong River. I sent Walsh with the company, and I took Hall and a light machine gun section to the left side of the North Korean's position. Bromser figured we would distract the North Koreans and help suppress their fire while the company advanced.

The hill was steep, and it took us a while to weave our way up the scrubby brush. I could hear the men straining against their loads. We'd almost made it to the top when I heard a single shot. Hall crumpled to the ground.

Everybody else dove to the ground. I crawled over to him. He was clutching his stomach and I could see blood seeping through his fingers. It had to be a sniper.

His skin was gray and he was in shock. Hall was in serious condition and we had no medic with us. I knew he wouldn't make it down the hill. I also didn't have men to spare, but I called over two of my new guys.

"Drop your ammo and get him back down the road," I said.

They rolled Hall onto a poncho and hurried down the hill, staying low and out of the sniper's sights. Without me saying a word, Heaggley took over Hall's squad, and we both picked up the ammo that had been dropped.

We kept moving up the ridge and into a depression protected by a knoll. The sniper kept shooting, but hadn't hit us again. Poking my head up over the lip of the hill, I called Heaggley and told him to move up to my position.

"Come around the knoll to the left and join me and the machine gun squad," I said.

The knoll offered some protection from the sniper. I crawled back into the hole and was lying on my back when Heaggley came over the top of the hill. I saw a puff of smoke right in the front center of Heaggley's helmet and he fell backward behind the hill. The sniper had shot him right between the eyes. I screamed for his squad to come around to the left, not over the top. I was waiting, but no one came. All of a sudden the first guy to come around the knoll was Heaggley.

"Jesus, Rich, I thought you hit me with a rock," he said.

Pulling off his helmet, he showed me the hole. It was square in the center of the helmet. The bullet had entered and followed the helmet around, taking a nick out of Heaggley's ear and cutting a deep groove into his helmet liner.

"You're a damn lucky guy," I said. But our smiles were short-lived.

One of the machine gun crew was not as lucky. He was dead.

From our position, we raked the North Korean positions with machine gun and 57 fire as the company charged up the hill. When the company joined us, the ridge was littered with the bodies of North Korean soldiers. We estimated at least two hundred dead, wounded or captured. We also found a massive weapons cache.

I saw a group of prisoners nearby. It was obvious that they had been in the field for a long time. Their uniforms were ragged and dirty. Caught in their holes or lying in front of our position, they had very little food on them. They were fanatical during an attack, but when we captured them they appeared childlike, very docile and scared. It reminded me of the photographs of the Japanese I had seen toward the end of World War II.

A few days later, we got the news on the Inchon invasion. General Douglas MacArthur conceived the bold amphibious landing far behind enemy lines on the west coast of South Korea in hopes of taking the war to the North Koreans. President Truman and the Joint Chiefs had reluctantly approved the plan, and the First Marine Division and the Army's Seventh Division went ashore on September 15.

The North Koreans only had about two thousand second-rate troops in the port city. The landing surprised the North

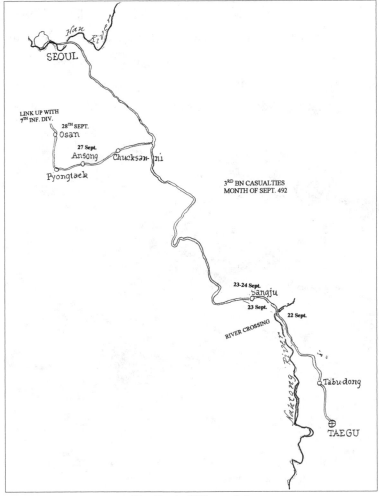

Timeline to 38th parallel.

Constructed by author based on daily battalion situation reports from the National Archives

Korean Army and they were quickly overwhelmed. Around Pusan, the impact was minimal. We had our own little part of the world to contend with.

Over the next few days we continued to attack to the west. It was a knock-down, drag-out slugfest. The North Koreans attacked us with abandon and tried to overwhelm us with numbers. They were fanatical. One regimental commander said after the war that the North Koreans had "no consideration for loss

8th CAV Regt. tanks and men close in on the enemy.
National Archives

of life. They have no hesitancy in losing five hundred lives to gain a small piece of ground."

It took us three more days to take two more North Korean positions. We uncovered large ammunition caches and killed seventy-two and captured two hundred. All at a great price. I lost two more men, and the company suffered a total of four killed, with thirteen wounded. The losses reduced our strength to around fifty-three men.

We were prepared to continue the attack, when we received orders to move to the road and start moving back east to the "Bowling Alley." When we got to the road junction, we saw that cooks had set up right on the side of the road and were passing out coffee and cinnamon rolls. It might as well have been a banquet. I never forgot the taste of that hot coffee and those cinnamon rolls.

The enemy was now on the run and we held the river line. The morale went sky high. We loaded on trucks near Tabu-Dong and headed north. Only three weeks earlier we had withdrawn south through the North Korean lines in the same vicinity.

Hard to believe.

CHAPTER EIGHT

PURSUIT TO THE 38TH PARALLEL

Hunkered down in my foxhole, I stared at the brownish water of the Naktong River and waited to cross.

For weeks, the river had been the line we had to hold, but now we prepared to cross it and finally take the war to the North Koreans. I heard the rumble of aircraft engines high above. I rolled over on my back, looked up, and there were six bombers flying low overhead. When they were a short distance from us, I watched as the bomb bays opened and to my surprise they released their bombs. It looked like they were going to drop them right on us. I was frozen in place as the bombs rolled out of the bay and sailed over the top of our position, crashing into North Korean positions on the other side of the river. I hoped they'd hit home since in a few hours I knew we'd be fighting through that area.

On the backside of the hill we occupied there was a pond. We could go down to the pond by platoon, and in my case section, and clean up. I peeled off my dirty and tattered uniform and waded into the bourbon-colored water. The warm pond felt great, and when it hit my thigh, I just sat down and let it swirl around me. Those brief seconds in the water were the best I'd felt in a long time. Standing up, I started to clean up. My skin was bruised and scraped. My joints ached, and after being on half rations, I was rail-thin. Wading back to shore, I pulled on clean fatigues from a pile left by the supply sergeant. Nearby, some of the guys were standing by a case of beer. Walsh saw me and handed me one. It was warm, he said, but tasted good. Greenlowe joined us. I handed him a beer. We both opened our beers and took a long pull. It was the best beer I'd ever tasted. I looked at Greenlowe to see his reaction; it was actually his first beer and he made a funny face. I slapped him on the back as Walsh and I both laughed.

Just before midnight, we headed for the ford. Engineers and civilian workers had built a pontoon bridge, and by the time we got there it was jammed with tanks, jeeps, trucks and men. As we walked along the road, we passed long lines of trucks waiting on the side. The drivers stood nearby smoking and talking. They knew what we all knew. This was the old Army game of hurry up and wait. We worked our way down the road and finally pulled off to the side near the river. It didn't bother me. I was clean, my uniform was clean, and I could still taste that beer.

At three the next morning, it was our turn to cross. We had a mission to capture and secure a small town a few miles north of the crossing site. As we hustled down the road, I saw what looked to be thirty North Korean artillery pieces lined up hub-to-hub. True to Soviet doctrine, they were massed and well forward. And caught totally by surprise when we breached their defense line. They looked like they were waiting for trucks or horses to tow them north. The tide had definitely started turning in our favor.

It felt good to be on the move. Pusan had felt like a merry-go-round, moving all the time but going nowhere. We spent so much time digging for our lives. Being on the move felt foreign and strange.

The road cut through some rolling hills laced with rice paddies. I could just see the village's squat huts in the distance. My eyes quickly found a high piece of ground just forward of the village and left of the road. That is where I'd be if I set up an ambush. All of sudden a North Korean machine gun started spraying the road.

They had us in the open.

Quickly ducking off the road, we started to slog through the dark, murky water of the rice paddies. The stench from the paddies was enough to choke a maggot. The mud at the bottom sucked at our boots, and the nasty stagnant water made some of the men gag. It was impossible to move quickly and we got bogged down there. At sunset, we were still in the rice paddies, between two roads. The North Koreans had us pinned down and unable to push into the village.

I heard the rumbling first. Peeking over the dike, I saw three Russian-made T-34 tanks. I could tell they were T-34s because of the narrow turret that sat at the top of the almost pyramid-shaped body. The tanks had led the charge against Nazi Germany in World War II. The T-34 dominated the German tanks because the Russian tanks could race over the deep mud and snow of the eastern front. After the war, the Soviets sold them to their Communist allies. The North Korean invasion was spearheaded by T-34 tanks.

The North Korean lead tank was almost on us. It stopped, and the main gun started to slowly turn in our direction. I looked at the road and saw a bazooka gunner jump out of the rice paddy, run to the middle of the road, stop, shoulder the tube and aim it at the tank. I thought this guy must have nerves of steel. It was a modern day David and Goliath.

Wham!

The rocket smashed into the tank and bounced off. The goddamn thing was a dud, or the gunner was too close and the rocket did not have time to arm. A burst from the tank's machine gun opened up and quickly cut the American gunner down. I scrambled down the muddy dike screaming at Heaggley to get his gun up. Machine gun rounds from the tank's gunner sprayed me with mud.

"Go for the treads," I screamed.

I watched Heaggley's assistant gunner slide a round into the 57 on his shoulder and tap him on the helmet. I slid to a stop and buried my head in my hands. I felt the concussion before I heard the round race by and hit the tank. The armored hulk tried to shake off the blast, but when it moved I watched the tread roll off the wheels. The turret still worked, and I could see it move back and forth searching for a target. Staying out of the North Korean's sights, I motioned to Walsh to get his gun on the second tank. In minutes, I heard another blast from the 57. Soon, the two tanks, unable to get by their crippled mate, reversed and headed back to the village.

We stayed crouched down and out of view of the tank's machine guns. I didn't want to expose myself. We didn't have any high explosive anti-tank rounds that could penetrate the tank's armor. We were at a standoff. With all the firing, I couldn't hear the American tanks coming up until they opened fire.

A pair of M-24s, primarily a reconnaissance vehicle with thin armor plates and a light 75mm cannon, came down the road and quickly blasted the lead tank with one shot. It was getting dark and the order came down to dig in. The stench and heat were almost unbearable, but it beat attacking the North Koreans at night. Our artillery continuously pounded them throughout the night, giving us some measure of confidence and security. We'd been on the receiving end of such barrages and knew how it frayed our nerves.

The next morning, we started out toward the hill and the village. A thick early morning fog hung low over the rice paddies. Visibility was zero. We were stiff, wet and very anxious as we started moving toward the objective. Up ahead, I saw soldiers walk through the North Korean positions and continue toward the village. Climbing up the last dike, we ran up on a road covered in North Korean bodies. They were in a heap, torn apart by shrapnel. Mules and broken equipment sat motionless nearby. Body parts were strewn on both sides of the road. I saw men lying dead still chained to the machine guns they were pulling. As the fog lifted, the sight became even more gruesome. Our artillery had caught them trying to withdraw. The same scene played over and over again as we moved up the road into the village. We didn't face a fight taking this position.

The company regrouped on the road and we were told trucks were coming to pick us up. The North Koreans were withdrawing so quickly that there was no way we could catch them on foot.

When the trucks arrived, we got a great surprise. The weapons platoon's vehicles also arrived. My section had two gun jeeps and I had a jeep and trailer. Two of the drivers were replacements for the section. I gathered the section around the first jeep and we spent the rest of the day going over how we operated mounted. Only Walsh, Hall, Heaggley and I knew we even had jeeps. The rest of the section had arrived after we left Pusan. Standing in front of the men, I realized that I knew very little about the replacements. And for most of them, I'd never know much more than their names, since they only survived a few days.

When nightfall set in, we started moving rapidly north. I tried to get some sleep by lying on the ammo backpacks in the trailer. I was half-asleep when I heard in the distance *"Banzai! Banzai!"* I leapt from the still moving trailer with my weapon at the ready. Squinting into the darkness, I saw some civilians standing near the entrance to a village. They were bowing and shouting.

"Manzai! Manzai!" Tony said as we passed.

Not *banzai*. I learned later that *manzai* meant welcome.

The North Korean Army was in total disarray. We grew leaders. Someone always stepped up and took over. They were followers. When their leaders fell, no one stepped up. They were isolated in their holes. Left alone, scared, tired, hungry and devastated. They were surrendering by the hundreds. We were simply directing them to keep moving south on the road.

Every mile we moved north my outlook changed. The whole section looked and acted more self-confident. When we got into a fight, we enjoyed it. The killing was quickly becoming revenge rather than a necessity to gain ground and drive the North Koreans out. We were still being killed, only now we were the aggressors and they were dying in their holes. I knew we were better fighters and had held under tremendous odds. Now the tables were turned, and they did not have the will or resolve to accomplish what we had in Pusan during the dark days of the summer.

A platoon of tanks was leading our company's advance until we hit some mountainous terrain. The tanks were having difficulty navigating the numerous switchbacks, so the company pushed up ahead with my section in the lead. As we climbed the mountains, we couldn't see around the bend in the road. After creeping around the first bend, I stopped the convoy and called Walsh over.

"Turn the lead jeep around and face the gun to the rear. Back around the corners," I said. "This way, we can get off one shot and if necessary scoot back to cover quickly."

Walsh smiled and turned the first jeep around. Looking at the road, he pulled the next one up so that we had two jeeps and two guns facing the enemy.

"Two quick shots are better than one," he said.

We continued through the mountains. I was a little more comfortable with this arrangement, but I hoped we would not run headlong into more T-34 tanks. In a few days, we'd almost made it to Seoul. Free from the mountains, we were close to pushing the North Koreans out of the south. Still in the lead, we overtook a North Korean headquarters unit that was trying to evacuate just south of the capital. I was near the back talking to Bromser and didn't get up to my section until after they captured the officers.

I saw Walsh and Heaggley standing by as some of the newer guys had the officers, high-ranking by the look of their uniforms, in the street. One of the officers couldn't stand and clutched his thigh. The others were leaning against a wall, hands high above their heads. They all were sharply dressed and well groomed. Obviously they had not been doing any of the fighting. I watched as my guys took their watches and other mementos from their uniforms. By the time I got there, all of the North Koreans had been ordered to strip out of their uniforms.

"Stop that shit. Let them put their clothes back on," I yelled at Walsh and Heaggley. "Make the men give them back their watches and get the wounded one over to me."

I called a medic up and told him to take care of the wounded officer. He was a colonel and wouldn't stop yelling at me in Korean. Between outbursts, he'd point and wave his hand at my men. I am sure like all officers he didn't care for being pushed around by soldiers. I ignored him and he finally shut up when the medic started bandaging his wounds.

I told Walsh to move forward and secure a bridge up ahead while I checked out the headquarters.

The wooden building looked like it was part of a small school complex. There was a total of four buildings. I entered one of them, and it looked like we'd caught them sitting down to lunch. The table was still laid out for the noon meal and some of the food was still warm. Lieutenant Bromser showed up soon after.

"It looks like we captured some kind of headquarters. We have about twenty-five prisoners and it's clear up to the bridge," I said.

Bromser took out a map and spread it on the table.

"I'm moving through with the rest of the company, and you can pull your men off the bridge and continue to get this mess straightened out. We're going to hold here for a while, and the battalion is going to come up and take the prisoners."

I ordered Walsh back and we tossed the headquarters. Throwing a table out of the way, we uncovered an open floor safe. It was stuffed with North Korean money. More money than I had ever seen in my life. The bills were worn and some-what ragged-looking. I couldn't read a single word, but on the back side they had western numbers. Most of the bills were one-hundred-won notes. The flip side had a picture of two workers. One held a hoe and the other a hammer. A few of my guys grabbed handfuls and stuffed them in their shirts. The money was worthless and soon became good for toilet paper or to burn and heat C rations.

We had orders to proceed to link up with the Seventh Infantry Division coming south from Suwon. We ran into them at Pyongtaek, a village south of Seoul. When we reached Pyongtaek, K Company from the Seventh Cavalry Regiment had already destroyed two North Korean tanks and cleared the village of North Korean troops.

We pushed north and passed through a Marine unit on the outskirts of Seoul. We continued on with the objective of occupying positions on the 38th parallel. The battalion was mounted in trucks and following a British unit. It was sometime in the afternoon when we started to move through the British. They were off on the side of the road in an apple orchard.

"Stopping for a spot of tea," we yelled at them.

The British started to shout back and laughingly threw apples to us. I remember the men in the trucks were singing "The Tennessee Waltz." We were having, as the British would say, a jolly good time.

It was impossible to predict when and where you'd run into North Korean troops. We were moving so fast that we'd overtake an enemy unit only to run headlong into another. It was hard to tell where the front was, which made moving stressful because behind every corner or bend in the road there could be a North Korean ambush.

We were now right on the 38th parallel and awaiting further orders. My section was covering a road. I had two guns, both on the left flank of the road so we could get good flanking shots at anything approaching. Right in front of our position there was a small village. I was a little leery of what was in the village. I decided to send Heaggley with three men to see what was going on.

"Get down in that village and get back before dark," I told him. "Watch yourself. There is no telling what's in there."

Heaggley took off and I watched with binoculars as he approached the village and disappeared. A few minutes later, he called over the radio that he didn't see any North Koreans.

"Keep looking," I said, and he pushed deeper into the village. Time went by and there were no more transmissions. I didn't want to call him because I didn't know his situation. But after a few hours, I started calling him on the radio. No answer. I was really worried now. It was dark and the company had no idea that I'd sent a patrol to scout the village. I knew I'd have to call back to the company soon so that we could put together a proper patrol to see what happened.

All of a sudden I heard Heaggley's voice.

"Jesus Christ, where have you been?"

"Rich, you are not going to believe it, we got into the village without any trouble, a couple of Koreans talked to us and said the North Koreans had left the village. We went into a house and the people wanted us to eat something. We had a little to eat and started to leave, and when we opened the door there were twenty North Korean soldiers out in the street," Heaggley said. "The people in the house signaled to us to be quiet and to stay inside. I didn't know what the hell the North Koreans were going to do. I just had to wait them out and hope when it got dark we could slip away. As soon as it got dark, the North

Koreans moved out and we slipped out of the village and directly back here. We never saw any more North Koreans."

"Shit. Where did they go?" I asked.

"No idea. But they left the village."

I called Walsh over and told him and Heaggley we had better keep an eye on that village tonight.

Early the next morning, we were back on foot, advancing toward the North Koreans behind three American tanks. We were receiving heavy artillery fire and I tried to stay close to the tanks, hoping the armor would shield us from the shrapnel flying through the air. One second I was looking back to make sure Walsh's squad was keeping up and the next I was stunned. A shell landed on the tank, sending shrapnel and fire into the air. The explosion was deafening and I stumbled back dazed.

Falling down in the tracks behind the tank, I saw the crew crawling out of the escape hatch. Machine gun fire was kicking up dirt all around me as I hugged the ground. I could see two tankers lying under the tank. They were wounded and couldn't crawl away from the hulk.

"Walsh," I screamed. "Help me get these guys."

A couple of artillery rounds landed on the road. I felt a sharp, hot pain in my left shoulder.

"Are you all right?" Walsh asked as he raced to my side.

"Yeah," I said, shaking my head trying to reassure him.

I didn't have time to worry about it. The machine gun rounds pinged off the armor as I crawled underneath the tank and grabbed one of the tankers by his collar. Pain shot through my arm and my shoulder felt hot and weak. I let go, but hung on with my good hand. Walsh grabbed the other tanker and we dragged the pair to a nearby ditch.

"Medic! Medic!" I screamed.

Blood poured out of their ears from the impact. Both men stared absently into the sky, almost like the blast had blown them far away from the hell around them. Walsh was urging his men to keep going. It was the only way to get out of the artillery fire. I left the tankers and kept the section moving out of the artillery.

With the two remaining tanks the company commander directed our assault on the hill to our right front. With the help of the tanks and our 57 direct fire, we took the lower portion of the hill. As we prepared to assault the North Korean position on the top of the hill, Walsh grabbed me. My shirt was now slick with blood from my shoulder. I could feel it trickle down my arm.

"What the hell are you doing?" he said. "Go get that shoulder taken care of."

"Quiet," I snapped.

I didn't want the rest of the section to know that I was wounded. I wiped the blood off on my pants and looked up at the hill. My shoulder burned, but there was no way I was leaving my men except in a body bag. Walsh wouldn't let it go. He was stubborn and kept after me. I knew that I would have done the same thing for him if he were wounded.

"Get a medic before we start up this goddamned hill," I said. "Don't say anything to anybody, understand?"

"Yeah, Rich, yeah," Walsh said as he went to get the medic. He looked relieved.

I squatted down and tried to take off my gear and jacket so the medic could get to the wound. My left hand shook as I peeled the shirt off, now a few shades darker from the blood. The medic arrived with Walsh. He wiped away the blood with a wad of gauze and started to bandage the gash. It was on the backside of my shoulder and I couldn't see the wound.

"A few pieces of shrapnel," the medic said. "You can move it, right? Probably nothing torn or broken."

The bandage felt good and I pulled my shirt back on. The attack was about to start. I saw the medic filling out a tag, a slip of paper put on each wounded soldier detailing treatments given and needed. A tag meant a trip to the hospital.

"Save the tag. I don't need it," I said.

A couple of days later, we sat overlooking the 38th parallel. We'd pushed the North Koreans back and now awaited orders to attack. My section was covering a road. I had set my two guns on the left side so we could get good flanking shots at anything approaching.

Sitting in my foxhole, I watched as the full moon began to rise. I got the feeling that there was something safe and secure as it washed gently over us. I felt like God was protecting us or surely trying to help. He'd at least kept me alive. My shoulder

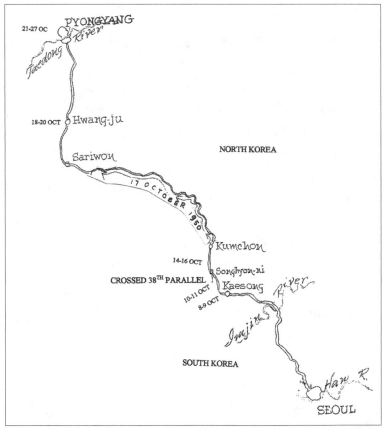

Timeline to Pyongyang.

Constructed by author based on daily battalion situation reports from the National Archives

throbbed, but I kept humming "On the Banks of the Wabash, Far Away" to keep my mind off the pain.

> *Oh, the moonlight's fair tonight along the Wabash,*
> *From the fields there comes the breath of new mown hay.*
> *Through the sycamores the candle lights are gleaming,*
> *On the banks of the Wabash, far away.*

If only we were back home, we could all go to sleep under the moon's calming light and wake up safe to the warmth of the sun.

CHAPTER NINE

THE GENERAL

I woke up and my shoulder was on fire. I could hear Walsh and Heaggley talking.

"You'd better get Vaillancourt up here," Walsh said.

I blacked out and woke up again in the back of a jeep ambulance bouncing down the road. It was dark and I had no idea where I was headed. I passed out again, and when I came to, the medics were transferring me to a box ambulance. I could see other litters with wounded soldiers. Holy shit, I thought, I must be being evacuated further to the rear. The last thing I heard was the rumble of the ambulance's engine before I passed out.

I woke this time just as they carried me into the battalion's aid station. The medics set the stretcher on a dirt floor. There was a medic leaning over me, and he spoke to me with a quiet, reassuring voice.

"You'll be okay, Sarge, I'll take care of you."

When I was thirteen years old, my old gang and I were down by the railroad with a bow and arrow. We were using the top of a peach basket for a target. We were shooting the arrows a hundred yards to the target that was placed on a hill. One of us would sit on the hill and collect the arrows that had been shot, then bring them back to the firing point and another guy would go to the hill. It was my turn and I was lying on the hill waiting to collect the arrows when I looked up and an arrow was headed right for me. I tried to roll out of the way, but the arrow dug deep into the calf of my left leg. The tip went right down to the bone.

I quickly pulled it out.

I was afraid to tell my mother and hid my injury for five days. I knew I would catch hell for being on the railroad, to say nothing of being stupid for lying on the hill next to the target. Soon, the wound was infected and I was forced to tell my mother.

When my mother asked how it happened, I lied.

"I fell on some reeds and one penetrated my leg," I said.

She did not buy my bullshit story and grabbed one of my buddies. He talked, and she scolded me all the way to the doctor's office, which was a few doors down. In those days the doctor worked out of his home. He propped my leg up on a table and took out what looked like a big green worm.

"You're lucky," he said. "Had you waited any longer, the infection would have spread."

I may have been lucky, but I didn't learn anything. I woke in the battalion aid station just as the doctor was cleaning out my shoulder wound. It wasn't infected, but he told me I was lucky.

For the next several hours I rested on a stretcher next to a wall with a large crack in it. I could see on the other side three or four South Korean soldiers. They were standing around a guy tied to a chair. They were working him over with what looked like rubber hoses. He was gagged, but I could still hear him moaning and trying to scream. I watched for a while and then turned my head and tried not to think of what I had seen.

I didn't know the facts. I knew the North Koreans slaughtered a lot of innocent men, women and children. I also knew some of the South Korean civilians had collaborated. I knew one thing for sure: It was out of my hands. But I still felt a little sorry for the guy.

The next day, I felt fine. The doctors still had me on a Jell-O diet, so when the doctor came on his rounds, I told him I wanted to leave.

"I need to get back to my unit," I said.

He shook his head. I pleaded with him. I was worried about my men.

"You leave, Sergeant, and you're on your own," the doctor said. "I am not releasing you."

I pulled my uniform shirt on and found the medic from the night before and got my rifle and gear. "Good luck," he said as I started north along the road. I had no idea how far I had to walk to get back to my company.

Not more than a half a mile down the road a military police jeep stopped me.

"Where are you headed?" asked the driver.

"Third Battalion, Eighth Cav," I said.

"Get in, we'll take you up the road," the driver said.

I jumped in the back, grateful for the ride. We got to a road junction and there was a steady stream of traffic moving in all directions. Long lines of trucks filled with supplies and troops, some towing massive artillery, crawled along the road.

One of the MPs walked over and talked to an officer standing by a jeep. He motioned for me to come over a few minutes later.

"The general's going to get you back to your unit."

"A general, holy shit."

The general was a tall, lean man with an air of authority. As I got closer, I could see one star on his helmet. It was Brigadier General Charles Day Palmer, the commander of the First Cavalry Division Artillery. A World War II veteran, he'd fought in the Normandy invasion, the breakout at St. Lo and the battles across France and the low countries to the Siegfried Line with the Second Armored Division.

"I understand you are a sergeant in the Third of the Eighth," he said.

" Yes sir. L Company."

"Just stay with me and I'll get you back to your unit."

He turned and grabbed the radio handset from his jeep. A battalion commander who'd missed his initial point (IP), the time when his unit had to move on the road, was on the other end.

"Colonel, is your executive officer there? Put him on the radio," Palmer said.

The executive officer came on the radio.

"Major, you are now in command of the battalion. I'm going to give you a new IP time. Do not miss it. Tell the colonel to report to my headquarters ASAP. Do you understand the message?"

"Roger that, sir," the new battalion commander said.

I also got the message: to never, ever miss an IP time.

"Lets go," the general said to me, climbing into his jeep. We skirted the road and drove up to his headquarters. The headquarters had just moved into what looked like a number of wooden schoolhouses.

When we stopped, Palmer called a sergeant major over to his jeep.

I didn't catch his name, but it didn't matter. When you're that senior, sergeant major is fine.

"Get someone to give Sergeant Richardson a haircut and then bring him to my mess for dinner tonight," Palmer said.

I sat down in a field chair outside, and the sergeant major talked to me while my hair was being cut. He told me that the headquarters just moved in and hadn't finished setting up security.

"We have a possible situation," he said.

"Yeah, what's that?" I asked.

"Do you see that high hill directly behind this building? We just moved in here today, and I am afraid there could be some North Koreans up there in that pagoda," the sergeant major said. "I haven't been able to get anyone up there yet. To be honest with you, my guys are not very good at taking care of things like this."

"Well, Sarge, what do you want me to do?"

"If I give you a couple of men, would you go up there and check it out?" he said.

"I guess so, if that's what you want, but who the hell does your security?" I asked. "The quartering party should have checked that out before you moved into this place."

He agreed. "I know, but they didn't, and now it's worrying me."

After my haircut, the sergeant major brought two of his

men to me. They were young privates and didn't seem too confident. These were not the battle-hardened soldiers from my section.

"Look, you men stay back and cover me as we move up the hill," I said. "Then while you move up I will cover you."

I took the lead up the fairly steep hill. When I got a ways up, I called the pair of soldiers forward. Then I moved out again. We did this five or six times until we got to the pagoda. Crouching, I approached with my rifle at the ready. I moved quickly to the rear. The pagoda was deserted and there was no sign of any recent activity. We stayed up there for thirty minutes. The guys with me had been very nervous and now looked relieved. The sergeant major thanked us and I made a point to personally thank the two men. There was nothing like a little excitement before supper.

The general's mess was in a room with a table set up in a U shape. The kitchen truck was backed up to a room next to it where the cooking was done. The general asked me to sit next to him at the head of the table. He introduced me to his staff and then called the mess sergeant over.

"Sergeant Richardson. Meet Sergeant Richardson." We talked for a few seconds and quickly established the fact that we were not kin. The general asked if I would like a beer.

"Yes sir," I said.

Then Palmer turned to his staff. "Let's let the sergeant eat, and when he's through we can ask him some questions," Palmer said. "You all need to hear what an infantryman's life is like."

The meal was some kind of meat, powdered potatoes and green beans. Good fresh-baked bread. The best thing was the cold beer. To tell the truth anything would have been better than the Jell-O diet at the battalion aid station.

When dinner was over, the general turned to me and told me to tell his officers what it was like in the infantry. Every staff officer was looking at me. This was a real chance to tell officers, including a general, what it was like and what we needed. I took a deep breath and then just told the truth.

"Look, I want you to know I'm not bitching, I'm just telling you the way it is with me and my men. My company strength was down to sixty-eight men and until recently we were fighting day and night. We have always been short of ammo. Most of the time we have been on one ration for two men and water has been a serious problem. Recently, we were given a box, which is called a 50-in-1, that contained a lot of razors, shaving cream, toothbrushes and toothpaste. Basically a bunch of stuff we didn't need. We need food and ammo."

The questions started right after I was done. They seemed genuinely interested.

How was the morale of my men through all of this?

"Since we broke out of the Pusan perimeter, it has been great."

Besides ammo and food, what else do you need?

"More artillery fire support."

They all laughed. When I left, they all thanked me and shook my hand. I never forgot the kindness the general showed to me. That night I slept in a building with wooden floors. During the night, I had a nightmare. I was in a hole and artillery fire was coming in on top of me. I dug deeper and deeper in the dirt with my hands. I couldn't get deeper because there were old boards in the way. When they woke me up, I was clawing at the floorboards. I looked around the room and the other ten guys in the room were up and looking at me, their eyes wide and scared.

"You all right?" one of them said. Even in the dark, I could tell I'd spooked all of them.

"I'm fine," I said. It took a lot of talking to convince them that I was fine. They still didn't believe me when they finally went back to sleep.

The next morning, General Palmer took me to my company. When I arrived, Vaillancourt met me.

"Great timing," Vaillancourt said. "A couple of men are being put on the promotion list, and if you were not here, we couldn't put you on the list."

I was being put in for promotion to sergeant first class. Vaillancourt told me that we had orders to cross the 38th parallel and move north.

When I got back to my section, I had three new replacements. Mac was a corporal and I assigned him to Heaggley's squad as a gunner. Allen had traveled with the circus and proved to be a resourceful guy. We were still short food, so he fixed a box to his ammunition backpack and I told him to pick up any discarded C rations. There were always items on the ground that had been thrown away. I told him that whenever we stopped he could make a mulligan stew out of what he picked up.

We were all saddled up ready to move out and two of the Koreans nudged me and pointed to McKee, one of the replacements. He didn't know how to put his gear together. Each step he took something fell on the ground. The Koreans were laughing. I got ahold of him and then I called Heaggley over and told him to take care of the situation.

The next day Heaggley came to me.

"Rich, it is impossible to keep him straight. He's going to get someone killed."

"Okay, I'll try to get him sent to the rear."

I went to Vaillancourt and asked that they send McKee to the rear, where maybe he could do something in the trains' area. They both blew me off. I figured as much. Heaggley would just need to keep a close watch on him and we'd hope to hell we did not get into a heavy firefight.

The battalion was attacking along open rice paddies. We were walking in single file on top of the paddy dikes. Heaggley's squad was in the center and Walsh's was on the right and just a little behind.

I was with Heaggley. All of a sudden there was a thunderous roar as an artillery barrage hit us. I was blown straight up in the air. My feet were over my head. I came down on my shoulder and my head. The mud softened the blow. Grabbing my helmet, I yelled for my section to run forward out of the kill zone. Three guys in front of me and two behind me were wounded. I could hear them moaning as they clutched their stomachs and legs. I checked myself; I had escaped without a scratch. Medics hurried to the downed men. I looked back and saw Heaggley standing dazed.

"Get moving," I yelled.

He looked at me with a funny expression on his face and then looked down at his waist. He had been hit by shrapnel in the stomach. I could see the blood soaking through his fatigues.

"I'm hit, Rich."

"Get down," I said. And I hollered, "Medic!"

Heaggley fell to his knees and rolled over on his back. I was torn. I wanted to run to him, but I had to keep the rest of the section moving. It was one of those choices that you never want to make. I saw the medics coming and turned to join the other men.

"Good luck, buddy. See you later," I screamed over my shoulder.

I couldn't look back, but I knew I'd probably never see

Heaggley again. A stomach wound, I thought, Jesus Christ I hope he makes it. I wanted to sit down and cry, but this was not the time or the place for that. I had damn near lost a whole squad.

We had to quickly reorganize. We were three quarters across the open area and took up positions behind a railroad embankment. I called Mac over.

"You're the squad leader and for the time being you're also the gunner."

Mac's eyes were as big as plates. He'd been with us less than two days.

"Any questions?" I asked, prodding him into action.

"I got it, Sarge."

I hollered for Allen and told him to get one of the Koreans. When they came back, I sent them to get the ammo we'd dropped in the rice paddies.

"Get there and back as quickly as you can," I told Allen.

They raced off and I turned my attention to the North Koreans. They'd dug in on the high ground two hundred yards to our front. There was only one way to go at the hill and it was straight forward. I looked across the open space we were going to cross. There was little cover. This was going to be tough. There was no time to dwell on Heaggley or on our dwindling numbers.

The longer we sat behind the railroad embankment, the

tougher it would be to get started. Bromser was waiting to get artillery support. The same guys I'd had dinner with. I hoped they remembered what I'd told them and come through. Leaning back against the embankment, I saw Allen and the Korean hustling across the field, each carrying two-pack boards with ammo.

"Get ready," Bromser said.

I gripped my rifle and closed my eyes. My mind knew going forward was crazy, but I willed my legs to move. Soon, I was running and leading the rest of the section across the paddies. Mortar and artillery fire crashed around me, but I didn't notice. I only saw the flashes of the North Korean machine guns ahead of me. I stayed close to Mac. I could hear him hollering at his squad to move. Looking to my right, I saw that Walsh was right beside us. He had his squad moving. It all seemed almost normal. It was just another day. Another attack.

Soon, we were in holes left by the artillery barrage. I could hear Walsh's 57 firing into the North Korean positions. Mac had his gun zeroed in on a North Korean machine gunner. After a few blasts, we joined our attacking platoons as they closed on the crest of the hill. My section moved up just in time to see the last of the North Koreans running away. For the next several days, each attack ended this way. It seemed the North Koreans were staying long enough to slow us down, only to run away as we got close.

During breaks, Walsh and I pressed Vaillancourt for information on Heaggley. When we got to the outskirts of Pyongyang, we finally got word. Heaggley was still alive when he was evacuated to the field hospital. That was good news.

On October 19, 1950, the First Cavalry Division was the first American unit in the captured city of Pyongyang. We'd been slowed after the North Koreans dropped all the bridges across the Taedong River. We added the North Korean capital to our legacy. First in Manila. First in Tokyo. Now first in Pyongyang.

The First Division of the South Korean Army entered the city simultaneously. They got the civilians under control. Pyongyang was a ghost city when we got there. We didn't face much of a fight as we walked down the wide streets.

We moved into an abandoned hospital. It was a disaster. Bloody bandages in heaps on counters and floors. Stained mattresses were thrown on the floors next to puddles of blood. All the equipment had been removed. The real horror was in the basement, where a hundred bodies were lying in piles.

We weren't there long before Bromser sent my section up to an outpost about five miles north of the city. We set up on a knoll overlooking a road and a railroad. I could see a steady stream of civilians shuffling along. I felt pretty secure since the North Korean Army was decimated. Just in case, I sent Walsh's squad down to the road.

"Make sure none of them have weapons," I said.

Turning to Allen, I told him to find us something to eat. We had C rations, but we were looking for something different.

"See if you can get us something to cook," I said. "And take one of the Koreans with you."

He came back an hour later with a big pot that they'd liberated from a farmer nearby and a bag of rice. The Korean was holding three chickens by their necks.

"How does chicken-and-rice soup sound, Sergeant?" Allen asked through a wide smile.

"Like dinner," I said and headed down to check on Walsh.

When I got to the road, I saw two of his men looking at a watch.

"What's with the watch?" I asked.

"An old Korean man gave it to me," one of them said. Since they were so new, I couldn't recall his name.

"What are you, stupid?" I asked. "Don't answer that. You probably scared the old man to death. Get Walsh over here. Damn it, hurry up and get him."

I looked at his partner. "Do you think this was right?"

He looked at his boots. "No, Sarge."

Walsh came up. He was shaking his head.

"Did he tell you about the watch?" I asked.

"Yeah, I'll take care of it, Sarge."

I turned and looked at the road. The Korean refugees had

nothing. Everything they owned was on their backs or in their bags. Men carried animals in cages. Women carried children. None of them looked at us. They kept their eyes forward. Scared. Beaten. Happy, like us, just to be alive.

"I hope the poor bastard will come through here again so we can give it back," I said. "This had better not happen again."

That night, we gathered around the pot and had the best damn chicken and rice. It was great and everyone had a full belly. Allen, the old roustabout, had cooked up a masterpiece. His time traveling with a circus paid off. We stayed on the knoll for a couple of days, until finally we got a message to pack up and move to Pyongyang. I sent Allen and the Korean to return the cooking pot to the farmer.

By now it was late October 1950. The North Korean Army was virtually destroyed. I'd been fighting since the summer, and for the first time I felt tired. Worn out. Standing in the formation, I looked out over the ranks. My unit was holding a memorial service for the 465 casualties the battalion had lost since August. So many new faces filled our ranks now. Only Sergeant Walsh and I had made it from the original section that had left Fort Devens.

Standing at the head of the formation, Colonel Johnson had a different message than the one at Fort Devens. This time he was somber, the losses having taken a toll. He was also leaving us, to take command of the Fifth Cavalry Regiment. As he spoke, I became lost in my own hurt feelings for the men that

I had lost, and I fought back tears. How tragic that these young men had their lives cut so short.

After the formation, I met with Lieutenant Paul Bromser and the other company leaders.

"Does anyone know how to load a ship?" Bromser asked.

We all smiled. That confirmed the rumor. The rumor was we were to be in Tokyo for Thanksgiving. And for me it meant maybe Christmas in Philly with my family. After the meeting, I went back to my section and pulled Walsh aside.

"Well, buddy," I said, "we made it. It's all over."

"What do you mean?" Walsh asked. I could tell he knew but wanted me to say it. He wanted to hear it.

"Looks like the rumor about Thanksgiving is not a rumor."

We stood there holding on to each other smiling and laughing like two kids. The entire section broke out in a cheer. Walsh and I made sure Tony understood the good news. He was the only Korean soldier left out of the original five assigned to the section.

Mac took four guys to the Bob Hope show that night. Walsh and I went to services.

Chaplain Kapaun had set up a makeshift chapel in one of the hospital rooms. He covered a small wooden table with a purple cloth and a chalice sat in the middle. Nearby was his worn Bible, the gold lettering on its black leather cover only specs after being carried from Pusan to Pyongyang. We huddled on rickety benches and bowed our heads.

"Heavenly Father, thank you for protecting these men as they did your work," he said.

I was not a religious person, but I felt like one that day. I gave thanks with Walsh for our gift of life. After services that evening we turned in our basic load of ammunition.

Another sure sign that it was over.

CHAPTER TEN

WE CAN'T HOLD
THE BRIDGE

That night, we got orders to move. But not home. We were headed north to the town of Unsan.

Early the next morning we drew our basic load of ammunition and loaded our jeeps and two-and-a-half-ton trucks. Soon we were bouncing up the road toward a city we'd never heard of and didn't care to see. Unsan sat in a wide valley north of Pyongyang. The valley narrowed in the south where my battalion was positioned. We stayed in reserve south of the city. The other two battalions were in forward positions slightly north and west of the city.

When we got to our company's reserve position, Vaillancourt took me aside and told me that I was going to be promoted to master sergeant. The company was shuffling some of its noncommissioned officers, and I was going to take the whole weapons platoon. Walsh, my best squad leader, was going to take the recoilless rifle section. He was a good leader and he never faltered no matter how bad the situation got.

I was a corporal when we arrived in Korea; now, less than

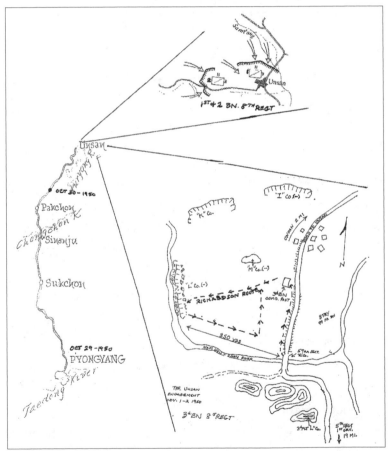

Timeline to Unsan. 8th Regt. Positions at Unsan. November 1–2, 1950.

sixty-seven days later I was going to be a master sergeant, the army's highest noncommissioned officer's rank. The promotions couldn't have come at a better time. With the war winding down, I was sure this would be the last of the fast promotions. Together Walsh and I had come a long way since Pusan.

The section was given the mission of securing the bridge at Camel's Head, and by midday we had moved to the bridgehead. High hills overlooked the south side of the bridge. The trees and bushes on the hills were more brown than green. That combined with a smoky haze that hung in the valley made everything looked gray and cold. It reminded me of the winter days in Philly.

When we got to the bridge, Walsh had the troops set up the guns while I looked around. The bridge was approximately ninety feet long and constructed of concrete. At its center it was about thirty feet above an almost dry riverbed. Two small rivers converged just east of the bridge, but at this time of the year both were almost dry. I noticed that troops could cross on foot almost anywhere and there were numerous places where vehicles could ford the river.

The battalion headquarters was four hundred yards north of our position on the left side of the road. It was in a dugout that appeared to be an old abandoned North Korean position. An artillery battery was about 250 yards to our right flank. We spent most of the morning digging in and positioning the guns. Since the company was close, we were going to be eating hot chow, good old shit on shingle and plenty of coffee, which helped since the weather was turning cold. Most mornings we woke up with frost on our ponchos and equipment.

Later in the day the supply sergeant, Sergeant Costello, drove up to the bridge with some field jackets and a couple of sweaters. He only had enough for half the men, so I told the squad leaders to make sure their men got taken care of first.

"Hey, is there any chance we can get a few more field jackets or sweaters?" I asked as Costello climbed behind the wheel of the jeep.

"I'll try," he said.

Costello started the jeep, and just before he pulled off, he stopped.

"Rich, listen to this dream I had last night."

In the dream Costello and his wife were old and he was dying. His wife and grown children were standing around the bed.

"You know what that means," he asked, ready to quickly answer the question. "Well, Rich, that means that I'm going to live to a ripe old age."

I smiled and put my arm around his shoulder. "That's great. Now go dig up some more field jackets."

Colonel Johnson, the new 5th regimental commander, had visited our battalion headquarters. On his way back to his regimental location he stopped at the bridge. I saluted and reported to him and he shook my hand.

"The Fifth Cavalry encountered a number of small North Korean roadblocks sixteen to nineteen miles to the south of your position," he warned me. "Be careful. I think they are isolated units and may try to withdraw up the riverbed."

Confident in my men and myself, I thanked the colonel for the warning and then said something I never forgot: "Sir, if they come up this riverbed, they've had it."

Johnson smiled.

"Be careful," he said.

As he drove away, I saluted and thought, Me be careful? You are the one who is riding back down that road. Despite my cockiness, Colonel Johnson's visit did put a new light on the situation. We now had to secure the bridge and be prepared to deal with the possibility of the North Koreans trying to move up the riverbed. We spent the next few hours shoring up our defenses. I had the men dig foxholes and positioned the two gun jeeps so they could fire north and quickly shift to the south if necessary.

Later that evening, I was sitting in my jeep, when, unbelievably, I heard the play-by-play broadcast of a Philadelphia Phillies World Series game. The 1950 World Series matched the Phillies against the defending champion New York Yankees. The Phillies—nicknamed the Whiz Kids—were a young team that had won the National League pennant in dramatic fashion on the final day of the season.

"Walsh," I yelled, not believing my ears. "Walsh, come here quick, listen to this."

One ball, one strike. The windup . . .

"Damn, Rich, this is crazy," Walsh said as we both started laughing.

We listened together, straining to hear the broadcast. The signal faded in and out, forcing me to move the radio up and down in hopes of picking up a clear voice through the static. The radios, for the most part, were pieces of shit. Most didn't work at all, and when they did they only had a range of about a mile. But that night I could hear the game just like I was home. For those brief moments, I *was* home, pulling for the Phillies, and not in Korea fighting for my life. Finally the signal was gone. I found out later it wasn't much of a series—Yankees in four.

"Can you believe that?" Walsh said, the smile still present.

"No, but I'm sure glad you heard it, because nobody will believe us when we tell them," I said, suddenly back at the bridge staring at the dark North Korean mountains.

The next day, I heard noises coming from the high hills across the river. It sounded like talking to me. I grabbed Walsh, and we walked to the south end of the bridge and listened. It was dark and quiet, but we could hear the murmur of several conversations.

"I hear it too," Walsh said.

I posted two men on the south end of the bridge, with orders to let me know if they heard anything. I only had a few men to secure the bridge, and I couldn't risk making contact with the enemy and getting split up in the dark. Returning to the north side of the bridge, I got on the landline back to the company and reported what I had heard. I asked the company for some help several times and after a while it became a plea.

Three calls later, a sergeant from battalion came down and reported to me. I told him what I thought was going on. He went back to battalion, then returned with three men and headed up the hill. They made the worst goddamn racket you ever heard. Loud talking, rocks and dirt falling all over and their equipment banging around. It was enough to wake the dead. If the Koreans were up there, the sergeant was not going to surprise them. Finally, they came back down the hill, making the same damn noise.

"Well, did you find anything?" I asked.

"No, there wasn't shit up there," the smug sergeant said.

"Goddamn it, something was moving around up there," I said. "I'm not losing my mind."

Walsh was standing next to me.

"You heard it right?" I asked Walsh.

"You're damn right I heard it," Walsh said.

One of the sergeant's men was holding something, but it was hard to make out what it was in the dark.

"What the hell is that?" I asked him.

"It's just an old glove and a shovel. It's all wet, and it's probably been there for weeks," he said in a defiant voice.

It didn't look like any glove I had seen before. It was large and padded.

"What else did you find?" I shot back.

"Just some old positions, nothing to worry about."

I was a little concerned now, and I continued to quiz him on how many holes there were up there.

"We found five or six," the sergeant said.

"Was the dirt dry or wet?" I pressed him.

"Goddamn it, I don't know. It was pitch-black. I'm telling you there's nothing on the fucking hill," the smug sergeant snapped at me. "If you don't believe it, you take your ass up there."

About that time I felt like taking the shovel and wrapping it around his head. I could see Walsh looking at me wondering what was going to happen next. It was all I could do to keep myself in check.

"Okay, just make sure you tell everything to battalion," I said, still absolutely sure I had heard voices.

When the sergeant was out of earshot, I pulled Walsh aside and asked him what he thought.

"The guy was too cocky," Walsh said.

I was worried and decided to keep two men on the south side of the bridge for early warning. I told Walsh we would stay in position with the rest of the men on the north side so we could protect the bridge and at the same time be prepared to fire on anyone coming up the riverbed. I went back to my jeep and contacted the company on the landline. I tried again to make the company understand my situation and my feelings about the patrol from battalion. This was bullshit and I wanted to make sure they knew it. At 2300 hours, the company told me to send a patrol to battalion. What the hell was going on? But orders are orders. I decided to send Walsh and his squad in one of the gun jeeps.

"Boy, Rich, that doesn't leave you with a helluva lot," Walsh said.

"Well I'll just have to think about pulling the two guys from the south side of the bridge," I said with a shrug. "Good luck and be careful."

"Same to you, Rich," he said, driving away.

At the same time Walsh was moving out, the artillery battery on my right flank cranked up and moved out toward Unsan. Now there was no one on my left or right flank. I was still not feeling very good.

Around 1 A.M., the hill erupted.

Four machine guns from the high hills on the south end of the bridge opened up, two guns cross firing on each end of the bridge. The tracers from the machine guns were skipping off the concrete like firecrackers. My guys quickly manned the 57 recoilless rifle and got off a few rounds. It did little.

Immediately, we started getting hit with mortar fire. My radio was shot up and I tried to get the company on the landline, but it was out too. My mind was on my men. I'd lost two in the opening barrage, and I had lost track of the two men on the south side of the bridge. This attack didn't make sense. Too much firepower for a few stragglers.

Lieutenant Keis, one of the platoon leaders, came running through the barrage. Unbeknownst to me, his platoon—the First Platoon of L Company—had been approximately fifteen hundred yards southeast of my position. Keis was out of breath and he wanted to use my landline. I told him it was out and I had no communications with anyone. He shouted to me that he was moving his platoon down the road to battalion.

As Keis headed off, I shouted to him that I was not sure how much longer I could hold my position on the bridge. He didn't hear me. The last man in Keis's platoon to pass through my position was Sergeant Miller.

"Good luck," Miller hollered as he ran by.

I had no idea of the tactical situation, so I called for Mac. I told him to work his way down the riverbank and try to make contact with the company flank. I needed to see what happened to the two men on the other side of the bridge. I told two men to cover me while I went under the bridge. I slid down the bank quickly, then ran through waist-deep water to the south abutment and started hollering. No one answered. I scrambled up the abutment and looked around. No one was there. I quickly made my way back, staying under the bridge. The machine guns were still raking the bridge with fire.

I was right at the base of the north abutment when we started receiving fire from the east side of the bridge. As I clawed my way up the bank, rounds were hitting the dirt all around me. The North Koreans were only thirty yards away. Luckily, Tony and another man were firing back. I made it to their position and joined them in trying to stop the assault. The North Koreans got within twenty feet, but we cut them down.

It looked like Fourth of July fireworks as the tracers skipped off the concrete, but I soon realized some of the fire was coming from our left flank. Jesus Christ, it was our own company firing on us.

I screamed at my men to keep down, don't return that fire. "Anyone see Mac?"

One of Mac's men hollered to me that there was someone coming.

"Mac, is that you?"

"It's me and I'm hit," he groaned. "Somebody help me."

"Keep moving. I am coming to get you."

There were tracers everywhere; everybody seemed to be firing. The only thing I knew for sure was that we were in trouble. I ran to Mac and helped him back into our position.

"Where are you hit?" I asked.

"My legs and I think my shoulder. Shit, Sarge, I'm not sure what's going on," he said, his eyes wide with fear. "I'm sorry I never got near the company. The Koreans were all over the place."

Mac was hit worse than he thought. I could feel his back. It was drenched in blood. He started to choke. I talked to him, but he didn't answer. I laid him down and at the same time hollered to the rest of the men to pull in tighter around the road. I had four men left. Our two jeeps were shot up. One was on fire.

I knew at this point we could not hold the bridge.

"Get the breech block from the 57 and throw it in the river," I yelled to my guys.

They scrambled off toward the gun. I took a waterproof bag that I carried in my pocket and placed my wallet, watch and all the information on the weapons platoon in it and buried it by the bridge abutment. I was not sure what was going through my mind at that point. I did know that I did not want the North Koreans to get any information off me.

The Koreans attacked again and got within twenty feet before we stopped them. I rushed to the other side of the road and got slammed to the ground from an explosion. Confused, I stumbled into a nearby ditch. My head was ringing. I checked Mac. He was dead, and so were the two other men on his side of the road. With only two men left, we had to leave the bridge. I shoved a grenade in the breech of the 57. The grenade exploded, destroying the gun. And we started pushing up the ditch away from the bridge. I couldn't see or hear anything.

We had not gone very far when the point man told me someone was coming down the ditch toward us. I took a knee and readied my rifle.

"Hold your fire until they get closer," I whispered.

The point man quickly yelled back.

"Sarge, they're our own guys. Two of them from battalion."

"Come over here. What's going on?" I barked to them.

The men look crazed. Both were talking a mile a minute and I tried to settle them down.

"Look, take it easy," I told them. "Slowly tell me what you know."

"The battalion got hit. They were in the headquarters before we knew it. The whole damn place was a mess," one of the soldiers said. "There were dead and wounded all over. Everything was shot up. It looked like an artillery barrage made a direct hit. It was total chaos."

"What are you two trying to do?" I asked.

They said they were trying to make contact with someone.

"Sarge, I'm Taylor, one of Walsh's men. The other guy is from battalion."

In the dark, I didn't recognize him. "Where's Walsh?"

"They're all dead, Sarge," Taylor said.

"Are you sure they are all dead?" I asked.

"I was taking a leak when all hell broke loose. The Koreans shot the guys right there in the hole they were lying in. It was really bad."

I had five men total. No heavy weapons and no idea what had just rolled over us. The firing slacked off but was still coming from all directions. I gathered the men up and made a quick decision.

"Listen up. We're going to move back toward battalion and hole up around the headquarters."

We got fifty yards down the road when one of the men saw movement.

"Sarge, there are some guys moving on the other side of the road."

I could not believe it. There were men walking in a column of twos. They were marching along like they were on a parade field. At first I thought they must be ours. They were coming from the area that the artillery unit had moved out of, but when they got close enough I could see their silhouettes. I knew they were not Americans. They had quilted jackets on and winter hats with flaps that covered their ears.

"Quiet. Get down," I hissed. "Stay down. When they get a little closer, fire when I do."

I took a deep breath and shouldered my rifle. All of a sudden everything was in slow motion and deadly quiet. I fired and put the first guy down. Seconds later we were all firing. Ten or twelve men fell to the ground. They never knew what hit them. Staring into the dark, we waited for movement. Any kind of movement. But it never came. The familiar rattle of an

American machine gun spitting rounds down the road finally broke the silence.

"Let me up front, let's move fast, come on, follow me," I barked.

Now we were in a trot. I knew we were getting close to battalion. Christ, there were bodies all over the place. I could see some men in the distance and someone yelled out.

"Over here to your left, come straight forward." It was a Corporal Jones hollering to us from behind a machine gun.

We stumbled into the battalion headquarters area and I introduced myself and asked Jones what the situation was. It was not good.

"There were thirty or forty wounded or dead. Doc Anderson and the chaplain are in the command post trying to take care of the wounded."

Jones thought the battalion commander was dead.

"They just walked in on them and shot up the whole damn place."

"How many men do you think you have?" I asked.

"Five or six."

"You got contact with anyone else?"

"No."

"Have the Koreans tried to get back in here?"

"Yeah, but we kept them away with the machine gun. They acted like they were just as confused as we were."

"I'm going to try to make contact with my company," I told Jones.

The company command post was dug into a nearby tree line, a quick walk from the command post before the attack. But now we had to make it through an open field with enemy soldiers all around.

"You're crazy, you won't make it across the open area."

I knew we had no choice. This position couldn't be held without help. And the only help was in that tree line.

CHAPTER ELEVEN

TRAPPED

"In the annals of modern warfare, there have been few units who have inked in their blood the gallant story of their last battle. They fought as the cavalry of old fought. The army can be proud of these men."

LTC. FILMORE W. MCABEE (NATIONAL ARCHIVES)

I checked my ammo and looked at my four guys. They looked nervous. I thought about leaving them, but I didn't know what I might find. For all I knew the company might have been overrun.

"Let's go."

They hesitated for a minute.

"Sarge, I want to stay here." It was the guy from headquarters. He was totally shaken and was looking at me with a blank stare.

I nodded and moved out. The other three followed. We'd barely made it into the field when the shooting started. We all bolted for the tree line. Jones was right. We were going to get shot up trying to get across this field. God, I hoped the company was there and not overrun like the rest of us.

"Richardson. Sergeant Richardson, we're coming in," I started screaming at the top of my lungs. "We're from the weapons platoon. We're coming in."

We got into the wood line and threw ourselves to the ground, completely exhausted.

"Where's the command post?" I asked between breaths.

"This is it, we are all here, the executive officer is right over there."

"Who's that?" First Lieutenant Frederick Giroux yelled.

Giroux had only been with the company for six days. A World War II veteran and experienced airborne infantry officer, he had taken control of what was left of the company.

"It's Richardson, sir, weapons platoon."

"How'd you get here?"

"Up the road to the battalion command post then straight across the field. The battalion command post is torn up, dead and wounded all over the place. I think the commander may be dead. I know the chaplain, doctor and about eight to ten men are still alive."

"Things aren't much better here," Giroux said. "The company commander is hit. We had a full-scale attack across our entire front, and before we knew what happened they were inside our position. It was total chaos. The best I can figure, we have twenty to thirty men."

Giroux asked if we could get out to the south. I thought a second and then shook my head no.

"We'd have to move past the bridge on this side for a good distance and then turn south. They have machine guns on the hills south of the bridge," I said. "We don't stand a fart's chance in hell of crossing anywhere near the bridge."

"How about east of the bridge?" he asked.

"I received a lot of fire from that direction, and later we shot up ten to twelve enemy coming from that direction, they were just walking in a column of twos," I said. "From what I understood that's the way they entered the battalion command post. A corporal at battalion told me that once they got into the command post they seemed as confused as our own people."

Giroux told me that once they got into the company position they got screwed up in the dark too. We were all running around in the dark, it seemed.

Giroux went off to tell Bromser about the bridge. I'd barely knelt down when some of the men, it was too dark to see faces, gathered around me. They were rattling off names of guys they knew were dead. The attack had run right through them and only 25 of the company's 180 men were left. Costello, the supply sergeant who'd just delivered field jackets to my section, was also dead. It was just yesterday he'd told me how he was going to live to a ripe old age.

Giroux called me over. He was sitting with Bromser, who had been badly shot up. There were no radios, and it didn't seem like the company had any communications with battalion or any higher units. The only information on the immediate situation was my report.

"We need to try to get out of here before daylight and move south," Giroux said. "Can you lead us across the field?"

"Yeah, I can. But we've got to watch that bridge and the machine guns on the hill," I said. "I've already been on the wrong side of those bastards."

Giroux looked at Bromser. It was clear he was taking on more of the leadership role since Bromser was wounded.

"We've got to go," Giroux said.

Bromser shook his head giving the ok to go. Giroux and I got everybody together.

"We're going to move out," Giroux said. "Take all the ammunition you can and take the machine guns. We move in five minutes. Sergeant Richardson is going to lead us out."

When everybody was ready, Giroux gave me the nod and I led us out of the wood line. I was confident I could lead them to the road, but I damn sure didn't know what we were in for when we crossed the river.

A thick smoke and fog hung over us, concealing our movements. I could barely see the hills. No one talked, but you could feel the nervous energy. After being run over, the last thing we wanted to see was the enemy. We'd made it halfway to the road when I saw two men walking toward us. Their weapons were slung across their chests and they didn't have helmets.

They were not Americans.

One of them saw us and reached into a bag hung over his shoulder and pulled out a grenade. I leveled my M-1 rifle and fired. The enemy soldier fell in a pink mist and dropped the grenade. It exploded, cutting down the second man, and shattering the silence. The explosion and flash alerted the machine guns on the hill. With deadly accuracy, the gunners started raking the formation. I tried to get the men moving, but panic set in. There was yelling and men running in every direction.

I could hear the roar of a tank engine and looked toward the battalion command post. It was two M4A3 Sherman tanks coming our way. I could see the green hulks moving toward us, a bright white star painted on their sloped armored fronts and the long barrel sticking out of the turret.

The men ran for them instantly. Where the hell did they come from? I thought as I ran toward them. I never saw them earlier as I moved through the battalion command post, and Jones, the machine gunner guarding the battalion command post, never mentioned them.

The first few men got to the tanks and climbed aboard. They saw the tanks as salvation. As Americans, we clung to our tanks for safety, a rock in the storm of machine gun rounds crashing around us. They figured the tanks could drive them to safety, but the men on top made it impossible to rotate and fire the machine guns on the turret.

The enemy machine gunners quickly zeroed in and raked the tanks with fire. I ran to the side near the track and started grabbing the men and pulling them to the ground. It took every ounce of energy I had to get the men off the tanks.

With nowhere to go, we started to dig in. The field was sandy loam that made it easy to dig trenches and foxholes. By daylight, we were dug into a perimeter 250 yards in diameter. Sergeant Elmer Miller, one of the tank commanders, moved his three tanks into the perimeter. I positioned the few machine guns we had at critical points along the trenches. We'd made it through the night, and the enemy rarely attacked during the day.

I was standing in a trench putting a machine gun in place when Chaplain Kapaun came along and asked me how I was doing.

"You know, Sergeant," the chaplain said, sporting his broken pipe, "it is All Souls' Day."

"I hope the hell someone's looking after our souls because we sure need it," I said back.

Kapaun smiled at me. "Well, He is, He is."

The chaplain moved on to another position, but before he left he told me we were fighting the Chinese. We'd heard rumors about Chinese soldiers coming over the border. That pretty much confirmed what I had thought for the last couple of hours. Jones had basically told me when he mentioned that their quilted uniform jackets looked so much different than the North Koreans'.

First Lieutenants Phil Peterson and Walt Mayo had also

scrambled into our perimeter. Both officers were artillery forward observers but had lost their radios in the confusion. They'd gotten reports hours before the attack that the Chinese were in the area. The Chinese soldiers had crossed the Yalu to protect electrical generators along the river. That night, Peterson had seen a Chinese prisoner in his quilted jacket but had no idea the danger we were in. They'd been ordered back to the battalion and then tried to escape when the artillery unit tried to save their howitzers. But the Chinese had already cut the road. We were trapped.

For the rest of the day, we set up our defenses. We knew the Chinese would come for us that night. Stragglers from the other units in the battalion kept arriving. By nightfall, we had about 120 men, with 50 wounded and approximately 90 dead. I moved around the perimeter checking on the men and tried to identify noncommissioned officers. None of the corporals or sergeants had any rank on their fatigues. It had been that way since we first exchanged uniforms in the Pusan perimeter. It was just as hard to find officers. They'd started pinning their rank under their collar because snipers were picking off the leadership first.

Some of the stragglers were from the mortar section. As they set up the 60mm mortar tubes, I quizzed them about Roberts and Vaillancourt. We'd been separated since arriving at Unsan, and I feared the worst.

"Both missing, Sergeant," one of them said.

The news hit me in the chest and nearly took my breath

away. I tried to stay focused, but my mind wandered to Pusan, Camp Stoneman, the train. To that damn infantry movie at Fort Devens. Walsh was dead. Now Roberts and Vaillancourt were missing. I was the last one. The only witness to the regiment being destroyed.

I kept circulating around the perimeter trying to keep guys focused. We needed so many things, but ammunition quickly became the most critical. I found out from one of the sergeants that the battalion had lined up all of the unit's trucks the night before the Chinese attack. We needed the ammunition in the beds of those trucks. I'd learn years later that all the rifle companies had been ordered to withdraw through the battalion headquarters area. My battalion was under orders to hold as long as possible and withdraw early in the morning. That was why all the vehicles had been lined up by the road.

I found Giroux near the tanks. He was talking to the tank battalion headquarters on a radio. Giroux called me over. There were bombers on the way; he wanted to call in an air strike and needed targets.

We knew that the Chinese were attacking us from three sides—east, west and south. After a short discussion, we decided on a riverbed in the east, the hill with the machine guns in the south and another riverbed in the west. There was still some vestige of hope. One of the last radio messages from division was that help was on its way.

While Giroux called in the details for the strike, I dashed

out of the perimeter toward the trucks. I knew the Chinese machine gunners were watching, but I hoped that one guy wasn't worth wasting the ammo. Running in a half crouch, I zigzagged my way out slowly, trying to take advantage of every little burrow in the field. It felt like forever before I finally got close to the trucks.

The olive-drab trucks were lined up on the shoulder of the road. Some were open and full of supplies. Others were kitchen trucks, mobile kitchens that could be wheeled to the front and cook hot food for the troops. I concentrated on the trucks with guns and ammunition.

I climbed into the back of one two-and-a-half-ton truck and started pulling open crates of ammunition and grenades. We needed both if we were to keep the Chinese off us. I worked my way through the bed of the truck as quickly as possible, trying to stay low. The Chinese must have spotted me, because suddenly I could hear the machine guns start firing from the nearby hill. Rounds smashed into the truck as I snatched up two large cans of ammo and stuffed grenades into my pants and fatigue jacket.

Diving out of the back of the truck, I raced back toward the perimeter. I could see the rounds kicking up debris all around me. Dropping the loot in a pile, I went back again. I played this game of chicken with the machine gunners three times before I couldn't stand any more.

At the end of my last sprint, my legs felt like jelly. My chest burned and I could barely hold the ammunition cans in my hands. I collapsed next to Giroux and Bromser in the trench. They had the grenades stacked up neatly in the foxhole we were using as a command post.

"Sergeant Richardson, let's keep the grenades here and pass them out only where and when we need them," Giroux said.

I just shook my head and leaned back in the hole. My fatigue jacket was soaked and my body felt weary, exhausted. I quickly recovered when Giroux patted me on the back. He didn't need to say anything. The moment was broken when we heard the rumble of the engines. They echoed as the planes approached from the south, dipping into the valley and flying over our position.

They were Australian bombers.

The planes came around low and fast and strafed the riverbed in the east. With their wings dipping low, the planes swung around and came right over our position again as they approached the hill south of the bridge where the machine gun positions were. Their guns sounded like loud zippers as they pounded the hills with long bursts. The machine gun links from the planes were falling right on us as they unloaded on the machine gunners who'd pinned us down. Every link increased morale. Everyone was excitedly waving and cheering them on. Pulling up after hitting the hill, they slipped over the mountains and disappeared. They didn't hit the west riverbed. Out of ammo, low on gas, who knows? As the saying goes, don't look a gift horse in the mouth.

Taking advantage of the attack, Bromser wanted to check out the battalion command post before the Chinese soldiers recovered. Operationally there was nothing left in the command post. The only communications we had were in Sergeant Miller's tank. I didn't think Bromser should go, but there was no stopping him. He wanted to check for survivors. It would be a treacherous dash fully exposed to the Chinese; however, the air strike must have shook the shit out of the Chinese. They never fired a shot.

Bromser and Giroux went into the command post while I waited outside and talked to Corporal Jones, who was still manning the machine gun. Jones was a medic from Massachusetts, and we mostly talked about home. I could tell he was nervous after manning the gun for so long. He'd kept the wounded in the command post safe and seemed grateful just to have some company. Anything to take his mind off things.

It's funny the things you find yourself talking about. He told me how he planned to join the State Troopers when he got back. I looked into his eyes and thought, Here's one hell of a brave guy. But I couldn't take my mind off our bigger problems.

Inside the command post, I knew what the officers were talking about. It was a forbidden subject. What were we going to do with the wounded in the terrible final moment that everyone knew was coming? The battalion surgeon, Doc Anderson, and the chaplain were doing what they could for about forty wounded men. But we couldn't hold out for long without a relief column. And if we had to run, the wounded officers were going to have to decide whether or not to leave themselves and the other wounded men behind to the mercies of the enemy.

Bromser and Giroux came out. They didn't say anything about their decisions and told me to get ready to head back to the perimeter. I knew this might be the last time I'd see Jones. He smiled as I stood up and waved. I didn't want to leave.

"Lieutenant, how about I come back with some men and help defend this position," I said. "Jones is beat, and if he doesn't get some help they will never be able to hold the position."

If they didn't let me come back, the Chinese would easily overrun the battalion position. It was a hard decision.

Bromser looked at Giroux. They knew the situation. They knew we were surrounded and trapped. You could see them doing the battlefield calculus in their heads. Could they spare anyone at their own position? Finally Giroux turned to me.

"Rich, you're coming back with us," he said.

I could see the pain in his face and I didn't fight him. I knew he hadn't made the decision lightly.

We moved back to the perimeter, racing through the open

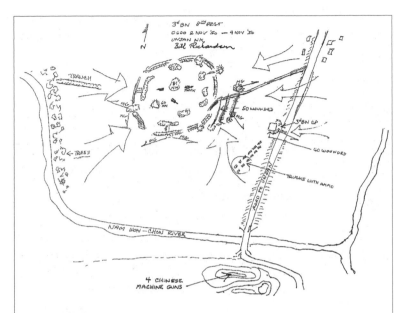

National Archives
Ltr. Dtd 19 February 1954 from Hobart R. Gay, Major General, U.S. Army
To Lt. Col Roy E. Appleman Office, Chief of Military History

"That evening" speaking of the evening of 2 November 1950, "at dark the Division Commander made the hardest decision he was ever called on to make in his life, that to obey the Corps order and abandon the 3d Battalion of the 8th Cavalry.

The whole catastrophe was caused by errors on the part of higher command, to include the Division Commander who should:

Have withdrawn the 8th RCT without referring to the Corps on the morning of the 1st of November.

Have never acquiesced to a night withdrawal"

Remnants of 3rd Battalion, perimeter defense. November 2–4, 1950. Excerpts from Major General Gay, 1st CAV Div. Commander 1950–1951. *National Archives* area but still not attracting the gunners. When we got back, I went to the west side to check on our defenses.

Wollack, a stocky sergeant, had taken charge. I never got his first name, we really just used last names, but I do remember he was Polish and one of twenty-six children off a farm from somewhere in the north-central part of the country. As we talked, I saw that a group of twenty men were running right at us. They were Americans and were hollering and waving at us. I prayed they were the lead element of a relief column. The others guys were cheering them on as they made the short dash to our trench. They slid inside, their chests heaving.

"What unit are you guys from?" I asked.

"Second of the Eighth," an officer said between deep breaths.

The stragglers pushed by us and collapsed in the center of the perimeter. Everyone's morale sank lower than whale shit. The energy and excitement seemed to deflate from the men in the trench, and all at once their heads hung and shoulders dipped. These guys weren't a relief column. They were just more stragglers from the Second Battalion.

I couldn't shake the thought that no one was coming for us.

CHAPTER TWELVE

DYING ONE BY ONE

The faint buzz of an L-5 artillery spotter plane shook me from my despair. I looked up, shielding my eyes from the sun, and could just pick it out. The olive green plane circled over us for a few minutes, then the pilot dropped two duffel bags out of the door and flew off. I watched the bags tumble from the plane and land in an open field about one hundred yards north of the perimeter.

I crouched at the edge of the perimeter and looked at the bags. Anyone sent out there would be exposed to the Chinese gunners on the hill. But we needed the supplies. And if we waited until dark, the Chinese would get them.

Without thinking, I dashed out of my hole. "Cover me," I

yelled over my shoulder. I tore across the field toward the bags, hoping to catch the Chinese by surprise.

No such luck.

I was nearly to the bags when shots hit all around me. I dove to the ground and crawled the rest of the way. I prayed that the duffel bags would be filled with ammunition and grenades. Grabbing one of the bag's olive green straps, I hoisted it onto my shoulder. The bag wasn't as heavy as I had figured but still weighed enough that I could only carry one at a time.

Taking a deep breath, I stood up and started running as fast as I could back toward the trench. Staying as low as I could, I dodged back and forth. Most of the shots cracked above my head. About halfway to the trench, a round hit the bag and almost knocked me down. I staggered forward and quickly regained my balance. Just as I reached the first trench, I stumbled and fell on some rocks. Two guys jumped out of the trench and dragged the bag and me to safety.

"You okay?" one asked.

"Yeah, I'm all right. What's in the bag?"

The soldier pulled open the bag, and medical supplies, mostly morphine and bandages, spilled out into the dirt. The other bag must be the ammo. I crawled down the trench, jumped out and ran like hell for the other bag.

This time the Chinese were ready.

Rounds were hitting the ground in front of and beside me.

They must be awful marksmen, I thought, just as a round ripped through the sleeve of my fatigue shirt and burned the hell out of my arm. I dove for the bag, snatched it up and started back to the trench. I was hustling with the speed of fright and dove the last few feet. I was spent and I sat on the ground trying to get my breath. My heart was pumping like it was about to jump out of my body.

Some of the other men opened the second bag and, like the first, it was filled with medical supplies. We needed the medical supplies, but we could not throw bandages at the Chinese. Giroux looked at me, smiled and shook his head.

Later that day, Wollack sent for me. I walked across to the west side of the perimeter and saw him standing near a machine gun position. He looked concerned and started pointing out toward what looked like an open field.

"Look over there," he said.

I watched where he was pointing. I didn't see anything. I looked at him and shrugged my shoulders.

"No. Keep looking," he said, this time staring intently.

Then I saw it. A faint shovelful of dirt flying into the air. The little bastards were digging a trench. There were about a half dozen or so digging a path right for us. Our machine guns had been keeping them at a distance. But when their trench was done, they could move under cover right up to the edge of our trenches.

"Jesus Christ. How many grenades do you have?" I asked.

"A couple," Wollack said through a scowl.

"Let me get you some," I said, still watching the dirt scoops fly into the air. "When they get close, frag them."

We were receiving harassing fire the whole time, but late in the afternoon the Chinese started to bombard us with 120mm mortars and rockets. We spent the rest of the day hunkered down in our holes as the explosions rippled through the ground. The Chinese focused much of the barrage on the tanks. One got hit and burst into flames. The tank crew and some of the other men managed to put the fire out.

Finally, Giroux told the tankers to move outside the perimeter. The mortar and rocket fire followed them. Tanks were made to fight and move, and in the perimeter they weren't effective. Low on ammunition and fuel, Miller decided to try and get out while the tanks could still fight. He ran back into the perimeter and told Giroux his plan. Giroux agreed, and just as it started to get dark Miller and the tanks moved out toward the road. That's the last we saw of them. Miller eventually had to abandon the tanks, but he was able to reach friendly lines on foot. He was the only one that got the message to our lines that we were trapped.

Sunset was a bad time. Night always meant another attack. It started with a probe. A few Chinese soldiers would move up to the perimeter, followed by a short and violent firefight. Shortly after the probe, the artillery and mortar fire would start, followed by the demonic bawl of brass bugles and whistles as the Chinese infantry attacked.

As soon as I heard the bugles, I raced to the interior foxholes and got the men up who could fight. I was getting aggravated trying to get the men to move out to the perimeter. We needed all the men and firepower we could get to stop the Chinese from breaching the line, because as sure as they breached it, we were done.

The men looked at me with weary and tired eyes. All of us had scruffy beards and our skin was caked with mud and blood. None of the soldiers could look at me. They knew that they wouldn't survive unless they got up and fought, but they just sat there. They were not cowards, just frozen by fear. For some, this was their first taste of combat. Boys who overnight were forced to become men. I could only imagine the terror they must have been going through.

"You've got two choices," I yelled. "Get up and get to the line or I'll shoot you."

That shocked them into action. I don't think they thought I would shoot them. I had no sooner finished prodding the men out of the interior holes than one hell of a fight took place at the battalion command post. I knew there were mostly wounded soldiers there and I feared for Jones, the lone man on the machine gun.

But I had my own problems.

The bugles and whistles broke the silence and the Chinese

rushed the east side of our perimeter. They came in waves straight into our fire. As quickly as they fell, more appeared. They moved into our fire like they were possessed. I raced from trench to trench, moving men where the Chinese concentrated their attack. When the attack on the east side slowed, they launched an attack on the west side. Although we were dug in, our casualties were mounting. I kept moving men to where the most Chinese were concentrated. The attack slowed down, but it was not long before they began an assault on the west side of the perimeter.

When I got there, Wollack had his men focused on the trench the Chinese had dug the day before. Each time a Chinese soldier popped out, Wollack's men quickly cut him down. I could hear the men screaming all types of obscenities over the roar of the guns.

Wollack suddenly burst from the perimeter through a hail of fire toward the Chinese. He hurled four or five grenades into the Chinese trench and dove to the ground as they exploded, throwing a plume of dirt into the air. Before the dust settled, Wollack jumped up and ran like hell back to our position. We waited for more Chinese, but they never came.

I grabbed Wollack as he scrambled into the trench. What he'd done was something out of the movies.

"We sure gave it to them little bastards," he screamed over the noise.

"You sure did," I said.

He was charged up. His eyes were on fire and he kept yelling at the now dead Chinese.

"You sure did," I repeated.

When I got back to Bromser and Giroux, I told them about Wollack and how well he was doing on the western side. But that was the only good news. We had very little ammunition left. The mortars didn't have any illuminating rounds, which lit up the battlefield so that we could see the Chinese coming.

Giroux was staring at the trucks just outside our lines.

"What if we shoot up the trucks?" he asked.

If we set ablaze the twenty trucks, it would provide enough light to see the Chinese making their way toward us.

"We have a few rifle grenades. I am sure along with machine gun tracers we will be able to ignite the trucks," I said, warming to the idea.

"Get them up here and get them ready," Giroux said.

I gathered up a half dozen men armed with rifle grenades and a machine gun crew with its tracers ready to fire when the next attack started. As soon as we heard the bugle, Giroux gave the order to fire up the trucks. We hammered the gas tanks and engines until they started to glow. Soon flames shot out of the cabs, engines and tanks.

When the Chinese infantrymen ran past, we could see them silhouetted against the light. It was a shooting gallery. We cut down the first wave only to watch the next one climb over their comrades and keep coming. We mowed down the next wave, but they still kept coming. For the rest of the night, the Chinese came at us like waves to shore. But each time we stopped them. They never reached the perimeter.

The next morning, I took stock of our situation. Water and food were a problem, but ammunition and the wounded were our biggest concerns. We had eighty-five able-bodied men left out of about two hundred. The rest were dead or wounded. We were also out of morphine, and the screams of the wounded were starting to have an impact on the rest of the men. I could see in their eyes a tired, haggard look.

"A relief column is coming for us. They'll get through today," I told the men as I walked the line. I said it over and over again, hoping to calm them and, as I realize in hindsight, probably hoping to convince myself.

I hoped to hell I was right.

When Giroux saw me walking the line, he called me over and asked me to go with him and Lieutenant Mayo to try and check the situation at the command post perimeter. I nodded and we quickly moved out.

Again, we made it without firing a shot. When we got there, everything was smashed. The Chinese had overrun the position. Every inch of the dugout was covered with the wounded. Only Doc Anderson was left. Also wounded, he hobbled over the men, trying to help. But he had few supplies and there was little he could do.

Between patients, he told us the Chinese had knocked out

Jones and the machine gun position with grenades. I left and started to look for Jones. I didn't really know the guy. But after our conversation a few days ago, I felt like I did.

The machine gun was gone. The bodies close by had been dead for more than twenty-four hours. Maybe Jones was still alive—somewhere. I went back to Giroux, who was still talking to Anderson. The doc said that when the Chinese got into the dugout, Chaplain Kapaun stopped them from killing all of the wounded by surrendering himself. The Chinese took him and fifteen of the walking wounded, including my old company commander, Captain McAbee.

"What Kapaun did was heroic, stopping the Chinese," Anderson said. "When he left, he was carrying Sergent Miller."

Miller was Gray's friend from Pusan. Standing in the dugout, we were all astonished by the chaplain's bravery. But Doc Anderson, I thought, stood in no man's shadow either when it came to bravery.

We left what food we had and went back to our perimeter. There was nothing we could do, and there was no way we could get the wounded back to our trenches. Plus, we already had more wounded then we could treat.

When I got back, I organized about a dozen guys to follow me out of the perimeter and gather up some of the Chinese weapons and ammunition. We were out of almost everything, but lying in front of us were weapons and ammunition, including much needed grenades. Before we left, I told the men to be careful because some of the Chinese might still be alive.

It was a gruesome business, but the only solution to our most pressing problem. Crawling over piles of dead Chinese, the smell was overpowering. At times, I could hear gas seep out of the decaying corpses. I could hear men behind me gag and throw up.

The bodies closest to our position had weapons and ammo. We quickly gathered up their rifles, including some submachine guns, which we called burp guns because of how they sounded when fired. But the farther we got from our trenches, the fewer weapons we found. I knew when the North Koreans attacked, their soldiers in the rear ranks would be unarmed. They would pick up weapons from the wounded and killed and keep moving forward. I wondered if the Chinese were doing the same thing, or if they just did a good job recovering their weapons and equipment.

For the rest of the morning, we passed out our new trove of ammunition and dug in deeper. As we worked, I heard the faint buzz of an airplane overhead. The spotter plane that had dropped the bags of medical supplies was back. This time instead of dropping supplies it dropped a message. And this time the pilot dropped it on target.

Giroux opened the message. I saw the color leave his face. I knew what the message said before he told me. We were on our own. No relief column was on its way. Our new order was simple. We needed to get back to friendly lines the best way we could.

While Giroux got the officers together, I gathered up a few sergeants and we had a meeting.

"Well we are on our own. That message told us to get back the best way we can," I told the sergeants.

Wollack was the first one to speak up. "We can't just leave the wounded."

"What the hell else are we going to do?" a sergeant I didn't recognize said.

The meeting was tense. I realized that what I had been telling them was going to happen wasn't going to. No relief. No rescue. And if we stayed in this hellhole we would all die.

"I don't think we can keep the Chinese out of the perimeter for more than one more night, if we can even do that," I said.

There was silence. We were facing death, but bravery is a funny thing. It comes in all sizes and shapes and appears in men you would least expect it from. Most of us didn't know one another, but we fought hard together like we were blood brothers.

"What do you all say about staying one more night? Maybe somehow they will break through to us," I said. "Tomorrow, we talk about the wounded."

Wollack nodded his head and looked at the others. "I'm for staying one more night."

Everyone quickly agreed. No one wanted to leave the wounded. I told Giroux the way the men felt, and after he met with Bromser, Mayo and Peterson, they all agreed. No one was comfortable leaving our wounded or the wounded nearby in the battalion headquarters.

That night the Chinese attacked three times. And three times we held, but not without suffering more casualties. After the last attack, I literally fell into a hole near the center of the perimeter. I was fighting a losing battle against sleep. I could feel myself slipping away. My body felt numb, damp and heavy. There was no noise, no sound. I was paralyzed, and the harder I tried to move, the more my body felt like stone. I tried to scream.

Nothing.

I tried harder. I couldn't make a sound. Was I dreaming?

I tried to relax and gain control, but I was beginning to shake. The ground was wet and I was cold. All of a sudden I heard voices in the distance coming out of the fog.

"Rich, Rich."

"Is that you, Walsh?"

"Yeah, I'm over here. Gray, Hall and Mac are with me."

"Jesus, Rich, it looks like the whole section is here. What's going on? What went wrong? What happened?"

I was trying to focus my mind. I felt like I was falling down in darkness. I kept seeing scenes flashing by in my mind. Where was I? What was going on?

What went wrong?

"Wait! Wait! Walsh, Hall, wait!" They were disappearing in the mist; it was very dark and I could no longer see them.

Oh God, I never had a chance to say good-bye or tell them how great they were, how proud I was of them, or tell them I loved them.

Bugles in the distance cleared my hazy mind.

I was confused and cold, but in a few seconds I realized where I was. The ground rumbled and explosions crashed around me. The Chinese soldiers were almost on top of us. The men were screaming obscenities, bugles were blowing. It sounds and looks like the devil bathed in blood should be dancing over our heads. How could sane men be engaged in this apocalyptic dance?

I could hear the *burp, burp* of the Chinese submachine guns, but not the constant rattle of our machine gun closest to me.

I instantly got a sick feeling. I bolted out of the trench and crawled toward the machine gun position and fell into the hole headfirst. The gunner was wounded and the assistant gunner was trying to put the gun back in action. There was ammo, but the gun was jammed.

I racked it back.

Nothing.

The headspace was screwed up.

There were Chinese within twenty yards of us and I was screaming for the men to keep firing. I pulled the gun into the hole and started to take it apart. I adjusted the headspace—put the barrel and chamber in alignment—and reassembled it. The assistant gunner laid the ammo belt in and slapped the cover down. I racked the bolt back and pulled the trigger. The gun jumped back to life. The fire immediately had an impact and drove a wedge into the advancing soldiers. The first burst took out half a dozen.

Some of the wounded and dead Chinese fell into our trenches. Others crumpled in a heap near the edge, close enough that we could reach out and touch them. I looked down and saw that the gunner was dead. The assistant gunner was hit in the arms and I could see blood staining his fatigue jacket, but he kept firing his rifle and replacing the ammo belts when the machine gun went dry.

Just as fast as it started, the attack ended. There was some sporadic firing from the other side of the perimeter. A couple of guys close to the gun position came over to me and took over. As I headed back to my hole, I crawled over several dead Americans and Chinese. Every trench and hole seemed to be full of wounded men screaming and crying for their mothers.

Always their mothers.

We had an added problem now since some of the wounded were Chinese soldiers. The dead were not a problem. We just pushed them out in front of the trench. But the wounded we had to help if we could. The medics did their best, but we barely had enough for our own men. The Chinese were all scared to death, crying and moaning.

They were the enemy, but they were also just soldiers like us, and it was difficult to see them that way.

CHAPTER THIRTEEN

BREAKOUT

The next morning, Bromser and Giroux called me over to them. The two artillery lieutenants, Mayo and Peterson, were also there. Giroux said what we all knew.

"We can't stay any longer. There is no doubt in my mind that the Chinese will overrun us tonight," he said. "We need to find a way out. Will you lead a patrol? Lieutenants Mayo and Peterson have already volunteered to go."

I looked at the lieutenants and nodded my head yes. Rank didn't matter and Giroux pulled me aside, put his hands on my shoulders and looked directly into my eyes.

"Mayo and Peterson are forward observers," Giroux said. "They are not infantry. You have the experience. Trust your instincts and find us a way out of here."

"Let me get one more man," I said and headed off toward Wollack's position. I wanted him to come with me, but he was focused on beating back the Chinese soldiers again building the trench. He was key to holding them off.

"I am organizing a patrol and need a good man. Got one?" I asked him.

He got one of his men and we met Mayo and Peterson. Squatting in a dugout, we decided to move along the ditch that ran beside the road and cross near a few Korean huts. The goal was to get to the riverbed where the Aussie bombers had strafed a few days before. We knew the Chinese had been using the riverbed to attack, but they were staying out during daylight since the bomber attack.

As we crawled down the trench toward the east side, word got out that we were going on patrol. Peterson crawled by a badly wounded radio operator.

"Lieutenant Peterson, where are you going?"

"Looking for a way out," he said.

"Lieutenant Peterson," the radio operator pleaded, "please don't leave me! Please don't leave me! You can't leave me here for them to get me!"

Peterson looked shaken and I urged us forward. I heard him say he was sorry as we crawled off.

Others reached out to us, patted us on the back and wished us good luck. McGreevy, a mortar man from the weapons platoon, called to me and handed me a pair of Soviet field glasses.

"Here, Richardson, you may need these."

Making our way down the ditch, we got to the crossing point near the huts. I poked my head up and scanned the other side with the field glasses. Chinese bodies were all over. Some lay on top of one another three deep. I imagined it looked like a Civil War battlefield.

"Cover me while I cross," I said. "Going to check out those huts."

I ran across the road and up to one of the huts. A few days before, we'd used it to store supplies. Sliding into the doorway, I burst through the door with my rifle at the ready. No one was inside the hut and I quickly waved the others over. We went around to the back of the huts and rushed through the doors searching for Chinese soldiers. The first two huts were empty, but the last one had two wounded Chinese lying on the floor. They had been shot several times and their breaths came in shallow wheezes. They held out their hands and started whispering what sounded like "shwee, shwee" in an almost eerie chant.

"Leave 'em," I said, not wanting to draw attention to us by lingering there. I'd learn later that the word was *shui*, Chinese for "water."

Using the rolling hills and depressions as cover, we continued to move toward the north part of the riverbed. Luckily, there were no Chinese around who were not dead or wounded. We got to the riverbed without incident and slipped down the bank.

Not more than one hundred yards away there must have been five hundred dead and wounded Chinese soldiers lying in the riverbed where our planes had caught them on the first day. Some of the wounds looked fresh and may have come from the previous night's attack. I could not believe they would leave their wounded lying there.

I called to the others and told them not to threaten the wounded. I was hoping that if we didn't threaten them they would leave us alone.

"Don't even look like you're thinking of pointing a weapon at them, let alone shooting one. Don't think about it. Those are the truest orders you'll ever get."

As we moved down the riverbed, the Chinese soldiers grabbed at us and held out cups begging for water. I took my canteen and turned it upside down to show them that we had no water. We had gotten about halfway down the riverbed when we all agree that we had seen enough. We needed to get the hell out of there, but it was hard to turn my back on so many Chinese soldiers. Even ones mortally wounded. All the way up the riverbed I was waiting to get shot in the back.

At the bank where we'd entered the riverbed, we stopped and squatted down. The plan was to move out of the perimeter just as it started getting dark so we could get through the riverbed before the Chinese moved in to launch their attack. Someone had to stay here and keep the riverbed under observation. This was the only way out of this hell and we had to make sure the Chinese didn't move in after we left.

Mayo and Peterson volunteered to stay while I went back to get the others. If the Chinese came, they would sneak back and warn us.

"Good luck," I told them.

As I turned to leave, I handed the binoculars to Mayo.

We couldn't go back the same way. I wasn't sure if the Chinese wounded in and around the huts had told their comrades where we'd gone. If we didn't make it back, the whole plan would be shot.

We went wide of the huts and followed a four-foot-deep irrigation ditch that ran toward the road, until we got to the field. Popping out of the ditch, we cut across the field full of dead Chinese, moving as fast as we could between the mounds of dead bodies.

As we entered the perimeter, the men were overjoyed to see us. Wollack's sergeant, just like scores of men I cannot remember the names of, had the guts to go on the patrol. We shook hands and he went back to the west side of the perimeter. I never saw him again.

I headed straight for Giroux's hole and went over everything with him and Bromser.

"If the situation changes in the riverbed, the lieutenants are to get back and let us know," I said. "If they don't come back, we have to assume the plan is a go."

"We move at seventeen hundred, before the Chinese move in," Giroux said.

Word was passed to all the able-bodied men. They were told to make sure that they took what ammunition they had left. I got a burp gun and some ammo. The wounded men knew what was happening. Some broke down, cried and begged us not to leave.

"Please dear God take us," one soldier begged me, grabbing at my shirt. "Don't leave us to the Chinese."

Others just watched us in silence. They knew they'd slow us down. They also knew that they'd be dead soon. They simply asked that we come back for them.

But I knew we were leaving them to die or, worse, get captured. I knew my orders and agreed with them. But I couldn't shake the feeling that I was leaving so many good men. Men who'd fought well only to be left behind to die. I wasn't sure I could ever forget this. This was to be the hardest thing I had done in my short lifetime.

We only had a few hours before we tried to break out. I wondered how the two lieutenants were. I guessed no news was certainly good news in this case. My heart was aching thinking of the men who would be left behind, when white phosphorous rounds started landing around us. They burst like fireworks, and the flakes landed on the wounded and burned through their uniforms. The screams of the wounded caused everybody to panic.

I looked at Giroux.

"Let's go," he said.

I stood up and gave the signal to go. I took the lead as the last sixty able-bodied soldiers moved quickly toward the old battalion command post. We then crossed over the road and headed for the river. It started to rain as we left. Smoke from the white phosphorous rounds and rain reduced visibility, giving us good concealment. We reached the river just as it got dark. Mayo and Peterson met us at the riverbed and we continued to move east. I was still leading the group when all of a sudden I saw movement to my right. I dropped to my knees, signaling the group to halt and get down.

I could just make out that it was another group of men. They also stopped and dropped to their knees. We weren't more than twenty-five feet apart, but I could barely see them in the smoke. They didn't look like Chinese soldiers. I thought I could make out the shape of an American steel helmet. My heart was racing.

"Who's there?" I finally asked.

The reply came back in English: "Who are you?"

Americans. We stood up and approached one another. It was the back end of the column. I didn't know we'd gotten separated in the riverbed. I quickly passed the word back, told the group to fall in on our group and I immediately started to move again.

A few hours into the march, the rain turned into a downpour. In minutes, we were soaked to the skin. The temperature was dropping and I started to shiver. Moving was the only way to stay warm, and I pushed on, trying to get as many miles as possible between us and the old perimeter. We were well behind Chinese lines, and because of the size of our group, it was likely we'd be spotted soon.

When we reached the main road, which a few days before we'd used to move supplies, it was clogged with Chinese soldiers. Some of the soldiers were on horseback moving south. Like us, they were using the road to move supplies and troops. Giroux and Bromser came up and joined me. We couldn't stay near the road for long. We had to cross quickly. We managed to string our guys out so that we could all cross at once. Hiding near the road, we watched for an opening. Finally, it came. We gave the signal and sixty men ran across the road as one.

After hours of marching, we finally stopped at a cluster of buildings. We moved the walking wounded who felt they could keep up with us into one of the houses and I spread the rest of the group out around the houses to watch for Chinese patrols. We were short on ammunition and I prayed we didn't run into any Chinese soldiers. We didn't have the firepower to hold out for long.

The officers got together in one of the houses. There were six or seven now, including Bromser and Giroux. Captain McClain, a company commander from E Company, was the highest ranking. With our security set, I went over to the house where the officers were meeting. I wanted to know the plan, but I got blocked at the door by an officer. . . . I asked for Giroux, who quickly came to the door.

"We're going to be here awhile," Giroux said. He seemed a little exasperated. I had a feeling we suddenly had too many chiefs trying to make decisions.

"We need to get moving and take advantage of the dark," I protested.

He shrugged. I left the house frustrated. Sergeant Mayer from the battalion's intelligence section called me over.

"Lets get out of here," he said. "You and I have a better chance to get back. This group is too large. We don't have the firepower to fight and they are slowing us down."

He was right. I knew together we'd probably make it back to friendly lines. Breaking down into smaller groups would be better. But I'd helped shepherd these men too far to turn my back on them, even if it cost me my life.

"Sorry. I can't do it."

Mayer shrugged and disappeared into the darkness. I went around the perimeter one time to make sure the guys were staying alert. We were wasting a lot of darkness. When I got back, Giroux and the officers were finally ready to move. This time, I was in the rear. Giroux wanted me to keep everybody moving. Many of us were wounded and weak, and as we walked over the hills the distance between the men grew. I was determined not to let them stop. I cajoled them along with encouragement and sometimes threats.

Just after daybreak, we were crossing over some hills when I heard automatic weapons fire. It was coming from the front. Everybody panicked and started to run. I tried to keep the group together, but it was impossible. By some miracle after moving a good distance from the firing, we were able to regroup.

We had just started moving again, when mortar rounds started to land nearby. The Chinese knew where we were now. We broke into two groups and started leapfrogging from one hill to the other. One group would cover while the other moved through. It was obvious to me that we were no longer evading. We were going to have to fight our way back to our lines.

By midday, the fire had slacked off and we were making progress. I could hear the rumble of artillery fire and guessed we were close to the front. My group climbed to the top of a knoll, and I could see the rounds hitting a mountain no more than five miles away. We were close. For the first time, I felt hope. Then the hill erupted with machine gun and mortar fire.

I was knocked flat on my face. I quickly got up and just as quickly got back down in the prone position. The Chinese were shelling the hill. My lower back felt wet, and I could feel what I thought was sweat running down the crack of my ass. It wasn't sweat. It was blood. I was hit, but I didn't feel anything. There was so much smoke, dirt and dust that I could barely see.

I stumbled off the hill followed by three others. We started running. The three men followed me. When we got to the road, I started following it to the east. We were running at a good pace over a little knoll when we ran smack into two Chinese soldiers. They were holding hands and skipping along the same path. One was holding a dead chicken by its neck.

For a split second we stared at one another. I shot the soldier holding the chicken. The other Chinese soldier went for his pistol. One of the guys with me shot him. Some Chinese soldiers nearby had heard the shots and were now chasing us. I looked down the road and saw an American tank sitting in an intersection about three hundred yards away. It was green and had a white star painted on the turret. We ran for it at a full sprint, but as we got closer, we saw that the hatches were open and there was damage on the armor plates. It had been knocked out days ago. I was panicked and needed to get my head straight.

There were about a dozen Chinese soldiers chasing us. I prodded myself to think and move. We started to head for a village on the other side of the road. Behind the village, I could see a massive rice paddy that ran up to a hill. I figured we could escape if we got over the hill first.

The paddy had about three or four inches of water in it. We stayed off the tops of the dikes and got halfway across the paddy before I turned to fire back. The Chinese soldiers dove for cover. When they did, we started running again. As I was running, I saw rounds hitting the water in front of me. When we got to the other side, we got down behind the dike and started firing at the Chinese again. I didn't see anyone behind them. If we could take them out, we had a chance. But the others didn't have any ammunition left and I was down to a few rounds myself.

"Get going," I said. "I'll hold them off."

They looked at me for a second.

"Go!" I screamed and turned toward the Chinese soldiers crossing the paddy. I fired a few shots and then dove behind a dike. A few seconds later, I fired two more bursts before I was out of ammunition.

Between bursts, my mind was searching for an escape route. I knew that if I ran straight up the hill, I didn't stand a chance. About thirty yards to my right, there was a house. A woman and a baby were crying and wailing in a dugout near the hill. If I went into the house, I was sure the woman would tell them. But I couldn't stay behind the dike with no ammunition. Jumping up, I ran behind the house and started up the hill. I tried to keep the house at my back hoping to mask my movement. I went as far as I could go without the Chinese seeing me and then dove into a large bush. Rolling onto my stomach with my Chinese burp gun underneath me, I waited. I had no ammo, but I had a death grip on the weapon. It was my security blanket.

I could hear the Chinese soldiers climbing up the hill. They were yelling at one another. I was trying not to move. Not even breathe. A fly hovered around my face, landing on my nose and mouth. I tried to close my mind to everything. I closed my eyes as they passed, and took my first breath as I heard their yelling behind me. In a few minutes, I was sure they were gone.

But every unit has one. A straggler that can't keep up. The Chinese straggler was so slow that when he got close to the bush, he saw me. I never moved and just shut my eyes. He started to holler and drove his bayonet into my butt. I felt the tip hit bone.

When I opened my eyes, I saw boots all around me. My mind went to the burp gun. If I rolled over holding it, they'd shoot me for sure. I shot my arms out along the ground and rolled over, leaving the burp gun in the mud. They reached down and jerked me up.

I wasn't going to be in Tokyo for Thanksgiving.

CHAPTER FOURTEEN

CAPTURE AND ESCAPE

The barrel of the pistol looked like the business end of a 105mm howitzer.

A Chinese officer with red piping down the sides of his pants had the pistol pressed between my eyes. He was screaming at me in Chinese and pointing up the hill.

I was numb and couldn't speak. I lifted my shoulders and let them drop. I've thought of this moment many times, and I know that if he'd pulled the trigger I would never have known it. That would have been the end.

The officer was puzzled. He jammed his pistol back into the holster, spun me around and kicked me in the ass to get me moving. They ran me back across the rice paddy, but halfway across my legs turned to rubber and I fell into the mud. What was happening finally hit me. I'd been captured and now I had no idea what to do. At least when I was on the run, I knew where I was going. Even fighting for my life was easier than giving up all control. I was now at the mercy of the Chinese.

When we got to the other side of the paddy, they tied my hands behind my back and threw me into the unused kitchen of one of the houses. I squirmed around on the dirt floor trying to get comfortable. The door opened and some Chinese soldiers started throwing corncobs at me. Others came in laughing and spit on me.

It crossed my mind that I had just shot up a number of them, and I wondered if they realized it. After a while they brought a couple more Americans and threw them in with me. Just as it got dark we totaled six. I knew none of them. Before I could ask any questions, the Chinese came and took us out to the road.

There were about ten Chinese guards. They lined up beside us and moved us down the road a couple of hundred yards. Suddenly, the one in the lead started yelling and the whole column stopped. The guards grabbed us and made us kneel down in front of a ditch. I could hear one of the soldiers barking what sounded like orders in Chinese. My mind went on full alert. They were going to execute us. I felt the guy next to me shaking, and another started sobbing.

My God, this is it. This is one of those situations where you expect to see your life flash before your eyes. I was ready to relive scenes from my childhood. Good times in Austria. Anything to take my mind from Korea and this ditch. It didn't happen to me. I just closed my eyes.

Instead of shots, I heard laughing. They motioned for us to get up. The guy next to me was so emotionally drained that he couldn't get up. I tried to help him, but my hands were tied behind my back.

"Get up," I yelled. "Don't let them laugh at you. Get up."

As they moved us on the road, we picked up more prisoners. By the middle of the night, we had about thirty-five in our group. I still didn't know anyone. We'd stopped earlier and the guards had loaded us up with captured rifles. When we got to what I assumed was some sort of headquarters, the Chinese marched us into the building and we stacked the rifles in a large room. I was dog-tired and my mind was working very slowly. I doubted that I had any adrenaline left in my body.

When we got done stacking the guns, the Chinese dropped a pile of rice on the ground and motioned for us to eat it. The prisoners rushed in and started fighting over the grains. I staggered back from the melee and angrily watched. We'd been turned into animals. After all we'd been through, why were the others not helping one another? Instead, they pushed and fought. I refused to join in. We needed leadership and control more than ever and I was going to begin leading by example.

I was about to start pulling guys off when a Chinese soldier holding a rifle led me and another soldier into an adjacent building. It was like a warehouse, with a massive open bay and dirt floor. The Chinese had set up two field tables, one close to the front and the other at the rear. A single candle on each table provided a little light, which made the room dark and sinister-looking. I was taken to the first table and the other man was taken to the back table. There were three Chinese soldiers at each table. One was seated behind. The other two were standing at his side.

The one behind the table asked me my name, unit and job.

"William J. Richardson, 13250752, sergeant first class."

I paused when I got to my rank. I wasn't sure if I had been promoted. The paperwork was in before we'd left for Unsan, but I wasn't sure if it had been approved. At this point, it didn't matter. The guy to my right started asking me questions. He didn't speak English very well, although I could understand him. He pointed to a map and asked me my unit and where I was located.

I laughed to myself. I had no idea where I was. I shrugged my shoulders and acted like I didn't understand. I wondered how long I could keep this up.

He asked me again. I could see he was getting aggravated.

"What unit you in? What you job? You tell me."

This time he didn't wait long for my shrug. I hadn't noticed a short, round stick lying on the table. In one swift movement, he had the stick in his hand and plunged it straight into my gut. When I bent over from the blow, he struck me along the side of my head, knocking me to the ground. Stepping around the table, he started to kick me. I struggled to breathe.

My mind jumped to when I was fifteen years old and out with my buddy Joe McMahon, who was two years older. We were drinking boilermakers in a seedy part of Philly where the bartender didn't give a damn how old we were as long as we had the money to pay. We got drunk as hell and I stumbled home around one o'clock in the morning. My mother met me at the door. She trapped me in the small entryway of the house and beat the hell out of me. It was classic do as I say, not as I do. I tried to protect myself, but I never raised my hand to her.

I knew I couldn't raise my hand here either. Luckily, one of the other interrogators came around the table and pushed my attacker away. They started shouting at each other in Chinese. Thinking about it years later, I figure he could have been praising the guy for softening me up. I had no idea what anyone was saying. I stayed in the fetal position trying to protect myself until the new interrogator helped me up.

As I got to my feet, I could see a gold crucifix hanging from a gold chain around his neck. He started speaking perfect English.

"Do not be afraid," he said. "He will not hurt you. That will not happen again."

My brain kept repeating, Don't be afraid. After a few seconds I realized the guy with the crucifix was talking to me.

"We are peace-loving people. We like the American people.

It is your government in Washington that is bad. Where do you live in the States?"

Without waiting for an answer, he continued.

"I went to school in San Francisco. Do you know San Francisco? I have many friends in the States. I had a wonderful experience while going to school there and I hope to go back someday. Someday when your government changes," he said.

Again without pausing for even a beat, he fired another question at me.

"Where were you born?"

Another beat.

"Are your mother and father living?"

I just stared at the crucifix and kept my mouth shut.

"Where do you live?"

He told me that we should be friends.

"Have you ever been to San Francisco?"

I kept staring. I was hurting and not responding to anything he said.

"I am a Christian," he said, "are you?"

I damn sure was now. I nodded my head yes.

"The Chinese People's Volunteer Army will not harm you, because we are a peace-loving people," he said. "We know you were being forced by your corrupt government to help the South Koreans in their invasion of North Korea."

Somewhere in the back of my mind I was thinking he

might get tired of bullshitting me and let me go. But as quickly as he started, he stopped.

"You go," he said and pointed to the rear door. "We will take care of you and I will see you again."

A guard took me outside and made me wait by the side of the road. One by one the others joined me. The temperature was dropping by the minute. I had nothing on but a fatigue shirt and pants. Others were lucky enough to have a field jacket. But we were all cold. I tried to focus on other things, but it was impossible. One guy, someone called him O'Keefe, started saying the Lord's Prayer in a thick Boston accent.

Finally, they got us up on the road and we started moving. We marched north in two lines, one on either side of the road. Chinese supplies and equipment moved south down the middle of the road. We were not moving very long when I heard rifle shots in the distance. The shots got closer until one was fired right in our midst. The Chinese started shouting, everything stopped, and the guards got us off the road into the ditches that ran alongside it.

Everything was quiet. I heard the drone of aircraft engines get louder and louder until they were overhead. American bombers headed north. After a few seconds, they were gone. Whistles blew and we were moved back on the road. It was not a very sophisticated warning system—but effective.

I knew one thing: Every step I took was taking me farther

and farther away from our lines. I had to get away and start moving south again. As this was running around inside my head, I heard the rifle shots again. It was pitch-black and I realized this was it. When the whistle blows, I am not moving. Like before, the whistles started soon after the aircraft passed over. But I didn't move. I stayed in the dark ditch and tried not to move.

I could hear the rest of the prisoners and guards move off. But within minutes, I fell asleep. I was jolted awake, and for a moment I didn't know where I was. I looked around for a second and it quickly hit me. I'd fallen asleep, and by the looks of the sky it would be morning soon. There was only one thing I could do and that was to crawl out of the ditch and get away from the road.

I crawled out and cut across a field. It was too dark to see much of anything, and I didn't know what kind of terrain was ahead of me. I got halfway up a hill with thick trees, but couldn't make it to the top. My heart was racing and I was wiped out. I leaned against one of the trees and immediately fell asleep. Sleep deprivation is a strange thing. Sometimes it's like turning off a motor.

The clanking of cooking pans and the murmur of hushed Chinese woke me. I looked up and saw hundreds of Chinese soldiers all around me. It was like sitting on an anthill. Way in the distance I could see the road and there was absolutely no movement. Then it hit me. The aircraft. The Chinese were afraid to move in the open during the daylight. There was no escape. I had no choice but to get up and walk out.

My uniform was covered in mud and almost unrecognizable. My face was also marred by mud and blood. I hoped they would be too focused on building fires and cooking to notice me. Standing up, I kept my head down and walked down a trail toward the road. My brain was screaming run, but I fought the urge. I just walked.

It almost worked.

I got halfway down the trail before a Chinese soldier started screaming at the top of his lungs. I looked for a place to run, but they were all around me. Two grabbed me and marched me back up the trail to a hut. They stripped me of my clothes, bound my hands and left me on the floor. I could see the guard's boots under the door.

There was no escape this time.

CHAPTER FIFTEEN

DEATH MARCH

The sun was starting to dip behind the hill when two guards came in and pulled me out of the hut.

Grabbing me under my arms, they picked me off the floor and shoved me out of the door. One of them barked an order in Chinese, but I had no idea what he was saying. I pulled on my uniform pants and shirt. My body ached and my back was stiff. I had to mentally force myself to take a step. I wandered out to the road. Five other Americans were standing on the road, flanked by three Chinese guards. I was put with the others. We didn't make eye contact. We'd lost our freedom and it hurt.

We started north up the road at a good clip. As we walked, I started to feel better. My legs felt strong.

"You guys been questioned?" I asked one of the Americans. Like me, he was filthy, with a few days of thick beard growth and dark bags under his eyes.

"Yeah," he said, not looking at me. His head was down as he focused on keeping up.

Damn. I'd been questioned once, but not by this Chinese unit. There was no telling what they might do when they found out I tried to escape.

Before long, we met up with another group of prisoners. It was a much larger group, about a hundred, and guarded by North Korean soldiers. The Chinese turned our small group over to their allies and left. Soon we were again moving north up the road. The guards circled us like sharks, pushing stragglers with their rifles, hitting and kicking anyone who stopped. Many in the group were wounded. One man had a massive chest wound. It was covered by bloodstained bandages. He wheezed as he shuffled down the road. My shoulder was a little stiff, and the shrapnel in my back was wet and sticky. But I felt lucky. It was nothing in comparison.

"Sergeant Richardson," someone said behind me.

It was Giroux. He had recognized my voice in the dark.

"Walk with us a minute," he said.

Bromser was walking nearby. He looked weaker and I didn't know how long he'd last. I wondered if Bromser had the strength to make it. Giroux said they'd been picked up soon after the mortar attack and marched north. As with me, the

Chinese had kept them off the roads during the day. They'd been fed some corn and water. Yesterday, the Chinese turned the whole group over to the North Koreans.

"We need to make sure we take care of Richardson when we get back," Giroux said.

"Yeah," was all Bromser could muster.

"Thanks," I said to the officers.

Before I could say more, a North Korean guard shoved me forward. I looked back over my shoulder. It would be the last time I'd see them. Fifty-five years later, I'd finally track down Bromser at his home in in Brownsville, Texas. We talked by phone and he told me Giroux died in the spring of 1951. The officer that was so strong and led us to safety just quit. He stopped eating. He wouldn't talk to anyone. Bromser talked to him about his children, but couldn't break him out of his funk. Giroux's life just slipped away. Bromser died a few years after my conversation with him.

Just before daylight, the North Korean soldiers shepherded us off the road and into a field. Waving their bayonet fixed rifles at us, they had us lie down on the frozen ground. The ground was so cold that it hit me in waves. I couldn't stop my teeth from chattering, and my legs and fingers turned numb. Staring up at the sky, I saw the last glimmer of some faint stars. I figured they were going to shoot us. But then North Korean soldiers carrying armfuls of cornstalks came out and started throwing them over us. The cornstalks were so that we could not easily be seen from the air. Lucky for us, they also trapped our body heat.

Many of us fell asleep. We were all exhausted. Huddled together, many of us spooning, we stayed relatively warm despite the freezing temperatures. By mid-afternoon, the cornstalks were frozen solid. I could hear the ice cracking around me as I crawled out of the cocoon. A few soldiers couldn't get up. Those of us who were stronger managed to get most of them on their feet. I grabbed one man, frozen in the fetal position, but he didn't move. He had died from the cold and his wounds. He looked peaceful. Farther down the row I saw them removing another dead man. My hatred for the North Koreans was growing greater by the hour.

While we waited to march north, two North Korean soldiers holding a basket moved between the ranks. When they got to me, they opened the basket and pressed a handful of boiled field corn into my hand. I slid the corn into my pocket, saving two large kernels. I tossed them into my mouth as we walked. I sucked on them until they were mush before getting two more. On my second two kernels, I screwed up and bit down on one of them, snapping a filling and breaking one of my molars in three places.

Pain shot through my head. My legs, back and shoulder were already hurting, but the pain in my jaw seemed worse. Probing the break with my tongue, I tried to keep the pieces of tooth together. But that only brought tears to my eyes. The pain was so sharp that I barely heard the English-speaking officer barking orders at us.

"Pick up wounded."

He kept saying it like a broken record.

Guards started pushing us toward the back of the formation. On the ground were about twenty soldiers on jerry-rigged litters made out of burlap bags stretched between poles. Ten more soldiers stood around them.

"Pick up wounded," the officer barked again.

It took four of us to carry one litter. I grabbed the closest litter and hoisted it up. The soldier in the litter had a horribly mangled leg. His calf muscle was long gone and his foot rested on the litter limp and lifeless. None of the wounded men had seen a doctor since being captured. I heard someone say they'd been in trucks, but were dumped on the road when the trucks were needed elsewhere. A whistle sounded and we started to shuffle forward. None of us were strong enough to carry the stretchers very long. My shoulders burned. I tried to focus on each step.

Left. Right. Left. Right.

Whenever things got tough, my mind wandered back to the guy with the sucking chest wound or I stole a glance at the guy on the litter with the mangled leg. I vowed to never quit, but soon my body started to break down. I tried to get another prisoner to relieve me. But everyone I asked looked away or moved ahead. Most hid in the dark, trying to stay as far away from the stretchers as they could.

"You son of a bitch," I barked at one soldier who almost jerked away when I asked.

I was disgusted. It reminded me of the soldiers that first night fighting over the rice. We'd forgotten that the backbone of any military was the bond of the soldiers. We fought for the guys to our left and to our right. That is why we fought. To protect our unit buddies, and we expected them to do the same. But on a death march, every man was an island. There seemed to be no place for anything else. I refused to be that way.

When I finally got someone to relieve me, I stayed close by and tried to get eight more men to stick close together so we could relieve one another. If we stuck together, we could make this march. Soon, I was back on the litter, and just when I thought we would not be able to take another step, we stopped. I could see the pink sky peeking over the mountains as the guards herded us onto the side of a hill. We sat in little groups huddled together against the cold. North Korean soldiers walked around carrying a chogie stick with a bucket of millet on each end. The millet was a fine grain almost like powder. As they passed, the guards slopped the gruel into our helmet liners. We didn't have bowls. Five or six men ate out of each liner.

We didn't have spoons and used pieces of wood instead. I found a flat piece of wood and sat down with my group to eat.

The millet was a pasty gray and had weevils and worms crawling through it. Some of the men near me started gagging and spitting it out on the ground nearby.

"I'm not eating that," I heard one soldier say, tossing his "spoon" away.

I shrugged and started scooping the millet into my mouth. I hadn't eaten anything except corn for several days. A few bugs weren't going to scare me off. I shoveled another spoonful into my mouth, careful not to hit my tooth. From that point, I ate everything I was given regardless of what was in it. Like before, we rested in the field, under the stalks, and were back on the road heading north just after sunset, again with a pocketful of corn.

Each night the guards were getting tougher. They were constantly pushing and hitting men with their rifles. If a man fell behind, he was shot and pushed off the mountainside. Everyone was rapidly losing weight. Lack of food, wounds and dysentery were taking their toll. Carrying the men on stretchers was becoming even more difficult.

We looked like skeletons. Our uniforms hung off us like a scarecrow's coat. Each time we topped one of the mountains, we faced another. Ears, nose, fingers and toes were becoming numb. At times I felt as though I was walking on my ankles. I was lucky that my legs had always been the strongest part of my body.

Many of the wounded men who were strong enough to

walk earlier now were in need of stretchers. However, there were none, and we found ourselves carrying them along between two of us. In some cases we were practically dragging them.

When I heard a single rifle shot back down the road, I knew another man's struggle was over. My heart was aching for them, but at the same time my mind kept telling me to move. We had two choices: march or die.

There was no doubt in my mind that during these night marches I could have easily escaped. The question was, escape to where? I knew that I wasn't strong enough mentally or physically. And with no map or idea how far I was from the front now, I wouldn't last long. My only choice was to keep marching.

My survival mode kicked in, not allowing me to surrender to pain and fatigue. When I could, I tried to focus on pleasant thoughts of home. I imagined baseball games I'd played in. I thought about my friends. My family. When I was eight years old, I'd get up in the dead of winter with no heat in the house. I would dress and walk a couple of city blocks to a store and get two bags of coal and one bag of charcoal. I would carry them back to the house and start a fire so that my brothers and sisters could get up in a warm room. I could almost feel the warmth of the fire on my face as I walked. When the good thoughts failed, I let myself retreat into a zombie state. My mind would black out, but my body would just keep moving until something snapped me back to consciousness. Like a snowflake on my face.

We were climbing up a mountain road. The snow made the road slippery. I saw a few guys slip, dropping a litter onto the ground. When we got to the top of the mountain, everyone was spent. It was hard to breathe in the thin air, and fighting the cold left us with little strength. My fingers were so numb I couldn't button my fly after relieving myself.

The guards shoved us into a cluster of huts. We were jammed into the room so tightly that my legs rested on another soldier. The only good thing about sleeping this way was that we were warmer. I heard O'Keefe's Boston accent reciting the Twenty-third Psalm in the darkness.

Yea, though I walk through the valley of the shadow of death,
I will fear no evil: For thou art with me.

As he said this prayer, a quiet came over the group. Afterward, I took off my boots for the first time in days. It was so cramped that I couldn't reach my feet. So I massaged the feet of the guy across from me and he rubbed my feet. We both put our boots back on, but a few guys left them off. We were all dead tired and had no trouble falling asleep. I woke to a bunch of guys raising hell.

"Where the fuck are my boots?"

"Get up! Get up!" the soldier yelled, so that he could look for his boots.

But we knew what had happened. When we went outside the hut, a few of the guards were wearing the boots. The North Koreans gave some of the men open sandals to wear instead. The cold was not only taking a toll on us, but also on the guards. A cold front from the plains of Manchuria came roaring down and slamming into the very mountains we were struggling through. We were facing the coldest winter in fifty years.

As we got ready to move out, the commander of the guards told us to leave the stretchers. The wounded were pleading with us to take them. I started to move toward one and got a rifle butt in the gut. Others tried to grab the stretchers, but the guards pushed them away too. I started to move toward the helpless soldiers again, but couldn't risk another blow. I let my mind drift into a zombie state, hoping to block out the screams of the wounded.

Left foot.

Right Foot.

Over and over again I repeated it until I couldn't hear their screams.

CHAPTER SIXTEEN

VALLEY OF THE SHADOW OF DEATH

After ten nights, we marched into a fairly good-size town wedged in a valley between the Kangnam and Pinantok mountain ranges. I heard the guards talking and finally figured out that the town's name was Pyoktong. It was early morning and a thick fog covered the tops of the mountains. As we approached, I could see numerous small streams cutting through the valley. A patchwork of turnip and corn fields spread around the outskirts and a few cattle mingled in a pasture. The cows were small and I could see their ribs.

The guards marched us to houses that lined the road. I'd just sat down on the dirt floor of one when I heard the hum of aircraft above.

"Americans, Americans!" I heard someone yell.

The hum changed into a screech as the planes started to dive toward the road. Everyone began to panic, even the guards. The buzzing of machine guns cut through the screech. Rounds started to rake the road and blast through the thin walls of the house. It sounded like a sharp pencil popping through paper. One of the prisoners in my house understood Korean. He was from Hawaii and also spoke Japanese, which many of the guards spoke as well.

"Let's take off," he heard one of the guards say.

"What about the prisoners?" another guard said.

"Screw the prisoners, let's go."

The guards outside of our house took off up the hill on the other side of the road.

We threw open the doors and followed. I looked down the road and saw all the prisoners pouring out of the houses. Searching the skies, I saw the glint of the aircraft turning around for another pass. We climbed up the hill as fast as possible, clawing at the dirt as the planes peppered the village again. As we reached the top, I heard a series of explosions below. The Air Force hit an ammunition storage area, and multiple explosions echoed across the mountains. All the prisoners were cheering and hollering.

"Hit the bastards again," someone yelled.

Thick black smoke curled up into the sky as the houses burned. I watched the planes climb high into the sky and disappear behind the clouds. Looking back at the town, I could see the bodies of a few prisoners near the houses. Others were wounded.

Numerous Korean soldiers started rounding up the rest of the prisoners. In the confusion, three of us slipped over the hill. We huddled together in a ditch, covering our hiding place with branches. We hoped to wait until nightfall and try to move back toward our lines. As we huddled together to keep warm, we talked about our chances of getting back .

"Any idea which way our lines are?" asked one guy. I'd never seen the other two soldiers. It didn't matter. We were all prisoners with one goal.

The other soldier and I shook our heads no. I sat back in the ditch and tried to get my bearings. It was hard because we had moved in during the night and the mountains now seemed to wall us into the valley.

"Well, we came from that direction," I said, pointing up the road that seemed to turn south. "I guess we could start that way and try to get over the mountains. We can use the road as a guide, but we will need to stay off it. All we need to do is keep moving south."

The older-looking guy with a healthy beard just shook his head.

"Suicide in our condition," he said. "We won't make it over those mountains. We don't have warm clothes and we will probably die of hypothermia."

We knew he was right. It was smarter to wait until

springtime. We needed to try to survive and hope our forces liberated us. A few minutes later, a Korean patrol spotted us in the ditch. None of us ran. We were all too cold and knew there was no place to go. The guards started to yell at us and quickly surrounded the ditch.

As they thrust their bayonets at us, one guard gestured for us to stand up. We stood, and he pointed back over the hill. They pushed us around a little as we climbed out of the ditch. When we got to the other side, we saw the rest of the prisoners together in a tight group. The excitement of the air raid was long since over, and now everyone's interest was in trying to keep from freezing.

The North Koreans seemed reluctant to take us back to the huts, so we huddled on the hill and suffered another frigid night. From above, our mass of men probably looked like a giant blob having a seizure. This time, we didn't have the cornstalks to keep us warm. We tried our best to stay huddled together, but the cold from the ground easily seeped into our bodies. I couldn't stop my teeth from chattering and barely slept. It wasn't until I was so cold that I couldn't feel my hands and feet that I finally got some sleep.

At dawn, they marched us down the road. But instead of back into town, we headed south. It was obvious they had no idea what to do with us. After hours of shuffling down the road, with one eye hoping to see the glint of more Air Force fighters, we stopped at a village. I figured we couldn't have marched more than a dozen miles from Pyoktong. The village sat deep in another valley. There were small farms of one or two houses stretching all the way up the valley for approximately two and a half miles. A small stream ran alongside of the road. It was completely frozen over.

As we moved up the valley, the Koreans started randomly splitting us up in groups and placing us in the houses. The guards crammed about twenty men per room in each house. Each farm appeared to have been one family's home.

The houses were made from wooden poles, with mud-baked walls and thatched roofs. Each house had three rooms, two bedrooms and a kitchen. The doors were covered only with paper and offered very little insulation or warmth.

It looked like the families that owned the houses had left in a hurry. Some of the farm tools were still there in open lean-to sheds beside bins of corncobs. Doors to the houses had been left open. Clothes, missed by the families as they hastily packed, littered the floor. I was placed in the last farmhouse. There was one other house beyond us, at the highest point in the valley, where the officers were held.

The valley was deep and the sun was only visible for three hours a day before it dipped too low on the horizon to warm the land. Temperatures hovered at freezing most days and dipped well below at night.

I got stuck sleeping near the paper-covered sliding doors. It was the coldest place in the room. One side of my body was always freezing. We were packed so tightly into the rooms that everyone had to move in unison. I was always happy when the decision was made to roll over.

The next morning five North Koreans crashed into our house. They threw open the sliding doors in both bedrooms and rousted us out. The leader, a stocky English-speaking officer with a clipboard in hand, started asking for our names and ranks. As we answered, they checked us off and moved on. When they got to me, the officer told me to come with him. I had no idea why. Did they know that I'd tried to escape twice already?

"You in charge," he said. "Everyone must stay in this area."

He indicated by pointing.

"You can go get water there," pointing to a nearby stream. "You understand?"

I nodded my head yes.

"Go inside," he barked. The rest of the group went back into the house, but I stayed.

"When are we going to eat?" I asked.

"Soon," he said.

The millet, which the guards brought to us twice a day, was running right through us. There was absolutely no nutritional value in it and no seasoning whatsoever. Everyone was losing weight. We were all beginning to look like scarecrows, some like walking death. Four or five men were still eating out of one helmet liner. Everyone was watching the other guy to make sure he did not get more than his share. We were slowly being reduced to the level of animals.

"We need medical care. We have men that are wounded and sick."

He said nothing.

"We need blankets and heat."

He looked up from his clipboard and gestured for me to go into the house.

"Go, go, go now."

I never saw that officer again. Our complaints and needs had fallen on deaf ears once again. I went back inside and tried to organize the men. I knew the North Koreans weren't going to take care of us. Sergeant Martin was the next highest ranked soldier in the house. I pulled him aside and told him he was responsible for the soldiers in the second room and I'd take care of those in the first room. I'd never seen Martin before. We didn't bother with first names or backgrounds. At this point, he and I were focused on living another day. I knew he was in my same situation, and that was good enough for me.

My goal was to bring back discipline and start acting like soldiers again. The scene the first night with the rice dropped on the ground was burned into my brain. The only way we could survive until spring and a possible escape attempt was to start working together.

"I asked the officer for food and blankets," I told Martin. "It remains to be seen if we get anything from him."

We walked out to the stream near the house. It was covered in a sheet of ice. Near the bank was a three-foot-deep hole where the Koreans got their water.

"Get a detail together and start getting water to the men," I said. "We can carry the water in the helmet liners."

Soon, three men were on the bank. Two of the men held the other by the legs while he went headfirst into the hole like a bucket in a well. Seconds later they pulled him up with a helmet liner filled with frigid water. I hoped the cold took care of the germs. I knew one thing: I didn't want to be here in the spring after hundreds of men had been defecating all over the place.

The Koreans took ten of us out under guard and moved us up the valley, where they told us to collect some firewood. We took the wood back to the house and the guards made us break it down into five piles, one to heat the house each night.

The house had hard dirt floors, and underneath was a small tunnel system that ran from the kitchen. Normally the family cooking in the kitchen would heat the floor of the house, but since we weren't cooking, no heat. That night, we took a pile of wood and started a fire in the tunnel. The heat in the floor only lasted half the night, but it still felt great. The lice loved it too. As I scratched, I thought of an old joke.

A guy goes to the doctor.

"I've got crabs."

The doc asks him if he has a lot of crabs.

"Well I've either got a lot or one on a motorcycle."

The sick and wounded suffered the most. Our frostbitten feet had turned to trench foot, and open wounds were infected or gangrene had set in. For those guys, it was only a matter of time before they died, since we had no medicine to treat them. I saw some of the soldiers turn to home remedies or even voodoo to treat their wounds. One guy took burned wood, scraped the charred area into powder form and swallowed it, thinking it might help stop or slow down the dysentery. Another one thought putting pine sap or turpentine on wounds would help heal them.

I tried none of it. I tried to clean my wounds every day. They were doing remarkably well considering I had no medication or bandages. I was keeping them as clean as I could. The shrapnel across my lower back was my biggest problem. I couldn't see it. I could only feel the shards and they were aggravated by the waist of my pants. But I was a lucky one. I healed quickly and none of my wounds got infected.

A couple of guys in the house were already sick. All of them were running a fever. Others, like a guy named Graves from Philadelphia, were bordering on pneumonia. He was nineteen years old and had just graduated from high school. Without any medicine, the only thing left was to feed his mind with good thoughts. My only hope was that if he stayed positive his body could fight off the infection.

We talked about all things Philly. We talked about meals at

Bookbinders seafood restaurant. Everyone from Philly knows Bookbinders. A city landmark, in the 1950s it was known for its five-pound lobsters and for being a place to see celebrities and sports stars. We talked over and over again about the lobsters' orange-skin shells. We talked about what we'd eat. What we'd drink. At times, I could almost smell the food.

If we weren't at Bookbinders, it was a block party. The police would close off one whole block and partygoers, bands, games, food and rides were set up. As with the restaurant, the memories were driven by our lack of food. Over the next month or so I repeatedly smelled the food, until I could taste what I was thinking about. We soon realized we were torturing ourselves.

As the days passed, he got worse until finally he stopped eating. I talked to him about his mother. I pleaded with him to eat so that he could leave when the American troops got to us. Anything to give him the will to keep going. Soon, he became delirious from fever and no food. He talked to his mother like she was in the room. He wailed at night. This spooked some of the guys. I saw a few lie with their hands over their ears.

Two nights later he died in his sleep. We took the body behind the house and dug a shallow grave. There were four of us in the burial party, and a man from South Carolina said a few words. We closed the grave and filed back inside. Everyone was silent. Graves was the first to die. Seven from our two rooms would soon follow him.

The valley had turned into one of death and suffering.

Soon after Graves's death, Chaplain Kapaun came to the house. We were all surprised to see him. I had last seen him at Unsan, but when he walked in I barely recognized him. The man I'd met on a ridge in Pusan was gone. He'd lost a lot of weight and his uniform kind of hung on his frame. His tired and worn-out eyes belied his warm smile.

"Where are you staying?"

"I'm staying with the officers in the house at the top of the valley," Kapaun said. "Dr. Anderson is also there and he is trying to get the Koreans to allow him to see the wounded."

The North Koreans were allowing the chaplain to move up and down the valley to visit us. There were about eight hundred prisoners in the valley. Kapaun spent about ten minutes in our house. Some of the guys asked about friends. Kapaun also told us who was dead or wounded. Before he left, he told us to get organized.

"We'll need to take action when the troops show up," he said. "Have a plan. When the troops get close, the North Koreans might try and kill us."

Kapaun believed our troops were close and it was only a matter of time before we'd be liberated. Before leaving, he promised to pray for each one of us. As he left the room and walked away, I stood near the house and watched him go. I didn't know if he was right about the troops coming or if they were close, but I felt good and couldn't wait until he returned.

Kapaun never came back to my house, but he continued to visit troops in the valley. I know he prayed for each one of us and when he could, brought food to the starving, until he became so weak that the guards took him to the hospital. He died of pneumonia in May 1951 and was buried in a mass grave by the Yalu River.

I took Kapaun's warning seriously, and the next day we started to watch the guards religiously, trying to understand their routine. The six guards that patrolled our house were all young and seemed nervous. Two guards each shift manned posts outside the buildings. They would holler at us when we moved too far from the house, but never came close enough to touch us. The goal, when the troops came, was to lure the guards to us and then overpower them. I tapped six of the strongest guys to be ready and to wait for my signal. I wanted to make sure our troops were close before we sprung the plan.

While out getting water one morning, I saw one of the guards bouncing up and down on the ground trying to keep warm. Each time he hit the ground, it gave like it was hollow underneath. I figured it was a root cellar and hoped there was food inside. Since we knew the guards' patterns, I waited until they were out of sight and dashed to the cellar and threw off the wooden board covering the door.

Inside there were vats of kimchi, a pickled dish of vegetables, mostly cabbage and varied seasonings. It stunk to high heaven, but it was better than the millet. Looking over my shoulder to make sure I was clear, I started to fill two helmet liners full of kimchi. I raced back and another soldier went with two more helmet liners. He was halfway back to the house when the guards appeared. They shouted and he dropped one helmet liner and ran like hell into the house. We waited for the guards to come. We could hear them talking and poking around the cellar, but they never came into the house.

"Maybe we got away with it," I said.

But I didn't feel that lucky. The next morning, the guards were at the cellar removing what was left of the kimchi. We usually got a bucket of millet, but this time we only got an English-speaking officer. He was small with a pocked face and dark, piercing eyes and an angry scowl pasted across his lips. I'd never seen the little son of a bitch before. He looked into the room and didn't say a word. We could feel his eyes on us. Finally, he started to call us one at a time back to the kitchen. I was one of the first to be taken out.

"Who took food? You tell me. You will not get food until you tell. You take food, no?"

I shrugged my shoulders.

"Nope," I said.

"You go back to room, I will get you again," he said. "You will tell who took the food."

When I got back, everyone was quiet. No one looked up at me.

"They're trying to figure out who took the kimchi," I said.

They all started talking at the same time in a machine gun burst of nervous chatter.

"Did they do anything to you?"

"Did they threaten you?"

I shook my head no. I tried to stay cool. Fearless. I knew the men were nervous, some scared. But I didn't want them or the North Koreans to see anything but cool.

"They are going to send for me again," I said. "That is what the little son of a bitch said."

Everyone got very quiet again.

"Don't worry. If I don't know anything, I can't tell them anything," I said with an almost cocky grin.

I kind of liked the little cat-and-mouse game the North Korean officer wanted to play. It kept my mind active and not thinking about food or home.

"But you know," one of the younger soldiers said.

"Shut up, asshole," Sergeant Martin snapped. He understood what I was doing.

Everyone sat quietly again. I wondered what I was in for and started to let my mind drift away, repeating over and over to myself that I didn't know anything.

"If I know nothing, I can't tell them anything," I repeated in a steady mantra. "If I know nothing, I can't tell them anything."

It wasn't long before the son of a bitch was back. He threw the door open and pointed at me.

"You come," he said.

I looked around and finally pointed at myself.

"Me?" I asked. I knew damn well he wanted me, but I wasn't going to come easily. I wanted the men to see me put up a little bit of resistance.

"You. You. You come." Now there was no doubt he wanted me. He took me back to the kitchen area and started the questioning all over again.

"Who took the kimchi?"

I shook my head again.

"Your guards took it. We saw them last night and early this morning. Go check."

Punishment for stealing kim chi.
Sketch by author

I could see the rage building up. He snatched his pistol and started waving it around like a madman. Oh shit, I thought. I was about to get shot over a few handfuls of pickled cabbage.

"You lie. You know and you tell me."

Eyeing that pistol, I figured I could take him and shove it straight up his ass. But there were two more North Korean soldiers standing behind me.

"Nobody eat until you tell me," he said.

They had not fed us that morning and it was getting late in the afternoon. I knew the men needed to eat. We were

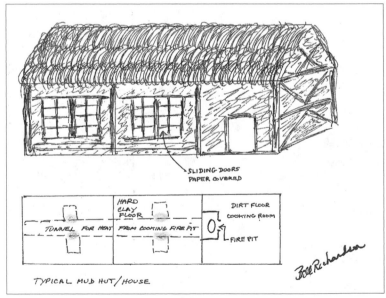

Typical Korean hut/house.
Sketch by author

weak and missing a day, even if it was that putrid millet, was out of the question. Plus, there was no telling how long they'd starve us.

"I did it," I finally said. "Only me."

Now it was the officer's turn to shake his head no.

"You lie. More do it."

"No. Only me and the guards," I said.

The little son of a bitch looked at me and then nodded to the guards, who grabbed me and tied my arms behind my back.

"You learn lesson now," the officer said.

The guards threw a rope over an open truss and pulled me

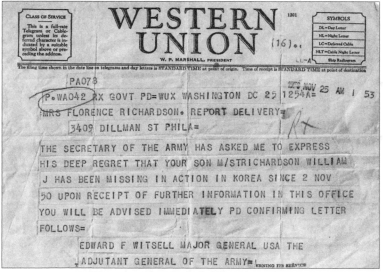

Telegram notice of missing in action status.

Author's collection

up by my arms until my feet barely touched the dirt floor. The pain was excruciating. I could feel lightning jolts of pain in my

DEPARTMENT OF THE ARMY
OFFICE OF THE ADJUTANT GENERAL
WASHINGTON 25, D. C.

IN REPLY REFER TO
AGPS-O 201 Richardson, William J.   28 November 1950
(20 Nov 50) 3446

Mr. and Mrs. William J. Richardson
3409 Dillman Street
Philadelphia 40, Pennsylvania

Dear Mr. and Mrs. Richardson:

I regret that I must confirm my recent telegram in which you were informed that your son, Master Sergeant William J. Richardson, RA 13250752, Infantry, has been reported missing in action in Korea since 2 November 1950.

I know that added distress is caused by failure to receive more information or details. Therefore, I wish to assure you that at any time additional information is received it will be transmitted to you without delay.

The term "missing in action" is used only to indicate that the whereabouts or status of an individual is not immediately known. It is not intended to convey the impression that the case is closed. I wish to emphasize that every effort is exerted continuously to clear up the status of our personnel. Under battle conditions this is a difficult task as you must readily realize. Experience has shown that many persons reported missing in action are subsequently reported as returned to duty or being hospitalized for injuries.

In order to relieve financial worry on the part of the dependents of military personnel being carried in a missing in action status, Congress enacted legislation which continues the pay, allowances and allotments of such persons until their status is definitely established.

Permit me to extend to you my heartfelt sympathy during this period of uncertainty.

Sincerely yours,

1 Inclosure   EDWARD F. WITSELL
 Bulletin of Information   Major General, USA
                                    The Adjutant General of the Army

Letter confirming status as missing in action.
Author's collection

left arm and shoulder where I still had shrapnel wounds. The pain quickly crept up my arms, driving straight to the top of my head. I gasped for air. The pressure on my chest only allowed me to take sharp short breaths. I could hear myself moaning, and once I cried out in pain before I passed out.

I woke up on the dirt floor. I could barely feel the guards pulling the ropes off my arms. I could hear the son of a bitch rattle off a few orders. He sounded far away, but I could see his boots and knew he was standing over me. The guards dragged me to my feet. Throwing open the door, they tossed me onto the floor of my room. I could barely move my arms and legs and stayed where I landed the rest of the night. Martin helped me get comfortable and told me that the house had been fed earlier that night. He had no idea how long I'd been strung up.

The next morning, I sat up and started making jokes. Some of them laughed with me. Others were just scared. Laughing hurt my ribs, but it was the first time I'd done it since Unsan. I was determined to keep my sense of humor. It was tied to my will to live. From that point on I remembered to laugh when I could.

"Well, I guess we won't be having kimchi anymore."

CHAPTER SEVENTEEN

REMINISCENT OF ANDERSONVILLE

After two months in the valley, the guards marched us out of the valley and back up the road to Pyoktong.

It was January. As we walked, snow started to fall. It felt good on my face and buried the valley in a white blanket. But the snow couldn't cover the memory of the more than three hundred men we'd lost. All of them died from neglect.

Instead of stopping outside the town, the guards marched us into the center of Pyoktong. The North Koreans and Chinese had moved hundreds of North Koreans out of their homes in Death Valley to make the first camp. They had done the same thing in Pyoktong, moving all but a few families out of the town and filling their homes with prisoners.

Like before, the guards separated us into groups and shuffled us into the houses. Almost all of the houses were wooden poles with mud baked walls, thatched roofs and dirt floors. Like in the valley, each house had three rooms, with paper doors to the outside. Again, we were packed tightly inside the two rooms. Winter was still with us and temperatures at night continued to drop below zero.

I was sitting on the side of a hill next to a house waiting for my assignment when another prisoner and I saw green stalks poking out of the dirt. I pulled one out of the ground. It was a wild onion. We dug up a few more and all of a sudden the guards screamed at us.

"No, you cannot have them," one guard said in garbled English. "Do not take more."

I was put in a house near the hill. The rest of the day, I kept an eye on the guards and the hill. The next morning, I raced over to the hill when the guards weren't looking and dug up eight more onions. I handed them to the guys in my house and dashed back to the hill to get more. I dug up another half dozen before I felt a boot slam into my back. Rolling over, I saw that one of the guards was standing over me screaming. He gestured for me to stand up just as two more guards arrived. One spoke English.

"We take you to the river," the English-speaking guard said.

I could see the men in my house watching as the guards shoved me toward the river. As we got close, one of the guards gestured for me to pick up a short log lying on the ground.

"Out on the ice," the English-speaking one said. "Hold log up." Showing how he wanted me to hold the log over my head.

I stood on the frozen river and hoisted the log over my head. It didn't take long before the pain in my arms overtook the pain in my feet. After what felt like an hour, I started to lower my arms. The guard immediately started hollering and gestured for me to put my arms back up. I tried to keep the log above my head, but I could no longer do it. I let it drop. The guard screamed at me to pick it up again. I was almost too weak to stand and I dropped to my knees. The guard was still screaming at me. I ignored him. I was on my knees, hands on my thighs, with my head down, when the guard delivered a swift rifle blow to my back that sent me sprawling flat on the ice.

"Stand," the English-speaking guard said, grabbing my arm. I walked with him off the ice and up the bank.

"You learned a lesson, no?" he said.

"No," I said, whispering "you bastard" under my breath.

The guard shoved me forward toward the house. Pushing open the door, he held me by the arm in the doorway.

"You see what you will get if you break rules," the guard said. "Do not take things."

He pushed me in and left. None of the others spoke. We all pretended it hadn't happened. That was a lesson that I'm sure was not lost on the men. But that night, I got a piece of onion. It was the best onion I'd ever tasted.

The Chinese finally took over operation of the camp in the spring. They were always running things from behind the scenes, but now they weren't hiding who was in charge. Chinese guards took over security, and political officers started coming into the camp. The Chinese issued each of us a small drinking cup along with a bowl for our millet or our maize. No more eating out of a helmet liner. We also were allowed to start a cookhouse for each company and were occasionally given soybeans.

We'd hoped that conditions would improve at this new camp, but little changed. Pyoktong had grown in clusters around deep wells that served a number of houses. But all of the wells were contaminated from animal and human feces seeping through the ground and into the well water, so we didn't have fresh water. The large prison population only added to the problem.

There were about three thousand men in the camp. Conditions were about as bad as a human being could possibly live with. This was about as close as you could get to Andersonville in the Civil War.

We were all full of lice. The farm boys told us they were hog lice, growing larger every day on our blood. While the lice got fat, we starved. The guards brought us two small bowls of millet a day and one bowl of boiled water, which barely kept us alive. And even when we ate, dysentery kept us weak and dehydrated.

Hunger can do some strange things to your mind. I was at the latrine—a slit trench—and I noticed that many of the soybeans were passed whole. I thought, Christ, if I picked them out of the feces and washed them off I could eat them. Then it dawned on me that I must be going crazy or turning into an animal. It would be a few days before I was able to get over the fact that I had let myself sink to a disgusting thought like that.

Soon after taking over the camp, the Chinese came in and ordered all sergeants to come outside. They wanted to separate the leaders and they marched us over to a new cluster of houses. At the same time, they moved all the blacks to a different area of the village.

As I got my stuff to move, I noticed the smart-ass from the battalion intelligence section who had led that noisy patrol near the bridge at Unsan. He was near the back and looked away when he saw me. Five of us got up and started to go outside. The battalion intelligence sergeant didn't move.

"Let's go," I barked at him. "Get off your ass and move outside."

"I'm not a sergeant," he said.

I shook my head. I knew battalion hadn't taken my warnings seriously. For a second, I thought back to Unsan. What if they'd sent a competent sergeant who patrolled correctly? Would we have found the Chinese before the attack? It didn't matter now.

"You son of a bitch," I said, glaring at him. "I was right about you all along."

Outside, I joined a group of about sixty senior sergeants. Without a doubt the best thing that happened to me was being put with sixty master sergeants and sergeants first class. I was the youngest of the group. As we walked, I struck up a conversation with a redheaded Irish sergeant. He had a prominent crooked nose and the weight loss made him look smaller than he was.

I introduced myself.

"Vincent Doyle," he said as we shook hands.

Doyle became the leader of our little group. An infantryman during World War II, he had a wife and a son in Fall River, Massachusetts. He'd received a battlefield commission in France and left the Army as a lieutenant. He opened up a frozen food store in Fall River, a little ahead of its time. Not many families had freezers. He went out of business and reenlisted as a master sergeant, not an officer. He was an inch too short to be an officer, the Army told him. We called him the "The Renaissance Man" because he seemed educated and wrote poetry. He carried a small red book with red Chinese characters printed on the top of the page. I'd catch him jotting down stanzas or quotes all the time. Sometimes, he'd read a few lines to me. One poem, "An

Infantryman's Troubled Dreams," was a favorite. Written in staccato sentences and observations, it seemed to capture the jarring experience of war.

> The din. The sweat. The blood of day. The agony of night.
> The roar. The shell. The scream of pain, the warriors'
> sad plight.
> An awesome tank. A sniper's eye. The hovering pall
> of death. A sig. A sag. A sprint. A dive. He gains
> another breath.
> The wet. The snow. The heat. The cold. A leg hurtling
> through the air. The noise. The quiet. The hurry. The
> wait. A head with blood matted hair.
> The sleepless eye. The bloodshot eye. The feet so stiff with
> frost. The endless march. The blistered feet, the heart-
> ache of battle lost.
> A meal. A shave. Mail new from home and cool water in
> which to bathe. Clean and fed, he lays his head to rest
> in a peaceful shade.
> Machine guns stutter. Sun on blades and so back into the
> strife. Attack. Patrols. Grenades and mines and he
> must risk his life.

Since we were a smaller group, I started to meet other guys in the house. We became sort of a family. On one of my first days in the house, I sat down next to Sergeant First Class

Smoak. He'd been with the Thirty-fifth Infantry Regiment and was wounded early on. The bullet had ripped through his lower buttocks and taken out his right testicle. We all cringed when he told us. But he smiled and kept telling us his story. He was evacuated to a hospital in Japan, recuperated, and went on a few days' leave. From his bed in Japan, he wrote to his girlfriend to tell her the bad news. But, as we'd come to learn, Smoak was always the optimist.

"Though there is one motor gone I can still carry on," he wrote.

For the rest of my time in that house, Smoak was the sunshine that kept our spirits up. Quick with a joke, he always seemed to be humming a few bars of "On Top of Old Smoky," his favorite tune. Smoak's mental outlook kept him strong.

O'Keefe was another World War II guy who got out and started a local truck business in and around Boston. He got tired of the trucking business and reenlisted. We'd been around each other off and on since the first night. It was O'Keefe who prayed that first night and said psalms during the death march.

Next to him sat an old Filipino sergeant. He was dressed in a hodgepodge of uniforms. He didn't say anything and just sat all day rocking back and forth and murmuring a lot of mumbo jumbo. As if he were a human metronome, you could keep the beat off his rocking. That and the mumbling used to drive some of the guys crazy.

O'Keefe used to blow his top at the Filipino. It always

started with O'Keefe telling him to shut up and ended with O'Keefe screaming it and stomping out. The old guy got on all of our nerves, and O'Keefe was just saying what the rest of us were thinking. O'Keefe was quick to apologize when he returned.

Our biggest problem was our physical condition brought on by the march. Men with open wounds, many with gangrene, didn't survive long. Some were saved from gangrene by maggots eating their dead flesh, which only meant they suffered longer.

Some of the soldiers had black feet from frostbite and trench foot. I watched while one man pulled rotted fresh off his toe bones. The soldiers from the Second Infantry Division had it the worst. They'd been issued shoe-packs, rubber boots with felt liners and insoles. Their feet would sweat and were continuously wet while marching, and they would freeze when they stopped marching. Since they never took the shoe-packs off, the soldiers got trench foot.

It is easily understood when men die of wounds or pneumonia. It was more difficult to understand when men just lie down and quit. I have seen strong men seemingly just give up and die. First, they would stop eating and stare with blank eyes at the mud walls of the hut. Their minds were gone, and life just slipped away. Then, after a few days, you heard an all too familiar death rattle.

We were dying at a rate of about thirty a day. Each morning, we took the dead out of the houses, stripped them of their clothes, and stacked them like cordwood in a pile. At first, we tried to take the uniforms and coats and give them to other prisoners, but the Chinese guards wouldn't allow it. What they did with the uniforms is still a mystery. For the most part, they sat in a pile.

We were required to provide men for a burial detail. The detail carried the bodies on makeshift stretchers made out of burlap bags stretched between two poles. It took four walking skeletons to carry each dead man across the ice. The ground was frozen solid. The detail would try to scrape a shallow hole and cover up the body with some dirt and rocks. At night, we could hear the wild dogs growling and fighting over the bodies.

I hated being put on burial detail. The physical part was bad enough, but the mental part was much worse. Thoughts about the families of the dead men and if they left children behind who might never know what happened to them. I knew from listening to men talk that what bothered most of them was the thought that they might be next. That's the one thing I never let my mind think about.

In a little more than three and a half months, sixteen to eighteen hundred men made the trip across the ice. One morning Doyle and I watched a burial detail. The dead were hanging off both ends of the jerry-rigged stretchers, heads and legs banging on the ground. Doyle turned and looked at me.

"Rich, if I go, promise me you won't let me drag along the ground like that."

"I promise you I'll make sure," I said.

How the hell could I do that? I wondered as I watched the ghostly parade pass by. I couldn't, because in my own mind I knew that within four or five days half of the men on the detail would be carried to their graves. We were all beginning to look more dead than alive.

Four or five days after the Chinese separated us from the others, I saw two political officers taking fifteen prisoners into a hut close to ours. I asked Doyle what he thought was going on.

"They're trying to get some men to write home and tell their folks how good they are being treated and that their families should tell our government to stop the war."

"Are you shitting me?"

"No, I'm not, Rich," Doyle snapped at me, and then he smiled and said, "Believe me, Rich, that's what's going on."

"Goddamn, we're stacking our dead bodies about fifty feet from that building. How the hell can anyone write that shit?" I said.

The next day, when the Chinese headed the prisoners toward the building, a bunch of us started shouting at them and telling them not to write letters. We repeated the same scene later when they left the building. This was one of the earliest attempts to use us for propaganda.

When I could, I went looking for Vaillancourt or Roberts. I'd been told that they were prisoners too. I was asking around a group of soldiers when I heard someone call my name. It was one of my guys, Elliott. He'd shown up just before Unsan. I'd sent him across the bridge before the Chinese attack and figured he'd been killed when they swept over the bridge.

"What happened Elliott? How did you get away from the bridge?"

He gave me a sheepish grin.

"I started to run back to the other side and about halfway I realized I would never make it and jumped off the bridge," he said. "I went up the riverbed to get away from the bridge and I ran right into the Chinese and that was that."

"Goddamn, that was thirty feet to the ground, you're lucky you could walk, let alone run."

"Yeah, Sarge," Elliot said.

I asked if he'd seen Roberts or Vaillancourt. Since he was a brand-new replacement, I should have known that he wouldn't know either of them.

I had started to walk back to my house, when I heard Roberts call my name.

"Rich," he said. "Rich. Is that you?"

He didn't look like the man I'd watched kiss his beautiful

wife good-bye. His face was thin and his eyes dark. He gave an awkward smile, but I could tell he hadn't had a lot to smile about. I could tell he was looking at me and thinking the same things. I no longer looked like the cocksure corporal who knew how to cut corners at the Fort Devens map course. We'd walked through hell and came out changed men.

"Boy am I happy to see you," Roberts said. "Val and I were both wounded and captured the first night the Chinese hit us. We were wondering what happened to you."

"Well it's a long story. I was just asking about you two. How's Vaillancourt?"

"Not too good, Rich," Roberts said. His shoulders sagged when he said it. Almost as if admitting it hurt.

"He's in bad shape. Hit in both legs. They both probably need to be amputated."

"What about you?" I asked.

"I got hit in my left arm and left leg," he said, rubbing his arm. "The arm is okay, but my leg is infected. But I'll be all right."

Roberts pointed out a cluster of houses down the valley where he and Vaillancourt were staying. He'd come up with some others to get water out of a well.

"Goddamn, you don't want to drink out of that well, it's contaminated," I said.

"It's okay, Rich," Roberts said.

"Bullshit. I'm telling you don't drink it," I said.

He laughed and waved me off. The others had the water in a few buckets and called Roberts over to carry a pair. They had been gone a long time and they needed to get back to their house.

"Well tell Val I was asking for him. I'll try to get to see you both later," I said.

It amazed me how fast our clothing deteriorated. Our boots just seemed to be falling apart. The seam on my rear belt line split down to my crotch, and the guys would laugh about my ass hanging out in the breeze.

Smoak pulled me aside one afternoon. "Rich, do you think you could get a couple of the boots before the Chinese get them?"

"What for? Most of them are no better than what we are wearing," as I looked at his boots.

"Just get a couple and I'll show you."

I worked my way around to where the Chinese had piled the clothing. I realized there was no use in thinking too much about how to do it; I just walked up, grabbed two of the boots and kept right on moving.

I headed right back to our hut and told Smoak.

"Goddamn, that was almost too easy. We need to think about stealing some of the clothes."

"Yeah," Smoak said as he grabbed the boots.

They were falling apart, and Smoak tore into them and

pulled out two pieces of spring steel. Each one was about one inch wide by seven inches long. Eventually some of the steel

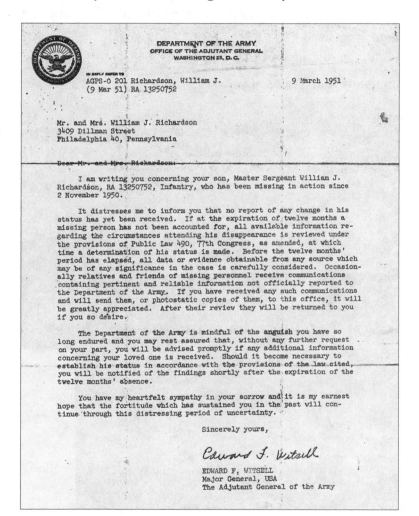

Letter dated March 9, 1951, reaffirming my missing in action status.
Author's collection

was honed sharp enough to shave with and trim our hair. My hair had grown long and hung over my neck. It, like my beard, was matted with lice. Shaving off the filthy hair made me feel human again.

It amazed me where I found and cherished little pieces of humanity in the camp.

CHAPTER EIGHTEEN

THE MORGUE

In early spring of 1951, the Chinese were building small docks on the river and I was unlucky enough to get put on the work crew.

The guards would march us out of town and up the surrounding hills to pick up huge timbers cut out of the forest. The timbers were used as pilings. In our physical condition it took twelve men to carry the thick logs back to the river. When we got them down from the hill, we had to move them three to four miles back to the camp. The work was hard, but it was better than the burial detail.

We'd been at it for about ten days. One afternoon, a group of us were carrying one of these timbers up a hill when someone in the center stumbled and the timber fell, pinning me to the ground. I screamed out in agony as the others tried to get the timber off me. The guards were raising hell, yelling and thrashing about. They seemed to think that I had caused the accident. The other prisoners managed to get the timber off me, and as soon as I stood, a guard struck me in the small of my back with his rifle butt, dropping me to my knees. The other prisoners quickly surrounded me, trying to protect me from other blows, but the damage was done.

I struggled to my feet and took my place under the timber, but my back was screaming in pain. I could feel the muscles tightening, and the shrapnel wounds across the small of my back were bleeding again. With every step, my back got more stiff. Soon, I couldn't turn or stand up straight. By the time we got back to camp, it was almost impossible for me to walk.

During the night, my legs from the waist down were hard as a rock and my lower legs were drawn up until my calves were touching the back of my thighs. My Achilles tendons swelled up as big as my thumbs and turned black, then blue and finally a sickening green color. The guys from my room carried me back and forth to the formations, and it was not long before the Chinese realized I could not walk. The guards came late in the afternoon a fews days after the accident. They marched into our house and hooked me under my arms and carried me out the door.

They were taking me to the hospital. We called it the morgue. We had never seen anyone return from there.

*   *   *

I wanted to fight back, but I couldn't. The guards opened the door to one of the rooms in the cluster of houses that served as the hospital and threw me in. It was dark and I could not see anyone. I landed on top of the wounded and sick lying on the dirt floor. They immediately started kicking and cursing me. The stench from the wounds and the human feces was unimaginable. I started to gag.

There was not enough room for the men who were already there, let alone me. As I wiggled around trying to find a space on the floor, a loud voice from the rear of the room boomed.

"Let him in, give him some room. Do you all hear what I said? Leave him alone."

The others made room and I finally sat down.

"What's your name?" the loud voice said again.

"Richardson," I said.

"I'm King."

King of the room or what? I wondered.

I was trying to cope with the odor and wondering if I was going to get enough space to lie down, when my diarrhea kicked in. But I was determined that I would not relieve myself right there.

"Where can I find somewhere to take a crap?" I said in King's direction.

"Out the door, go left to the end of the building, left again, and twenty-five yards on a knoll you'll find the latrine."

The temperature was freezing, but I welcomed the fresh air. I dragged myself out on my buttocks, pushing myself along with my hands. I reached the latrine, a trench a foot and a half wide and ten feet long. The trench sat just outside a strand of wire that separated our camp from the black prisoners.

The human waste was like pudding and almost reached to the top of the trench. I managed to get my pants down and had worked my way to the edge, when the side caved in. I fell into the trench, finally catching my shoulders on the edge. The waste was at my chin as I clawed at the dirt trying to pull myself free. My paralyzed legs, like an anchor, pulled me toward the bottom. I yelled out and kept clawing, but every second I slipped deeper and deeper into the trench.

Two black prisoners on the other side heard me. They crawled through the barbed wire, grabbed me by my arms and pulled me out. A second later, and I would have slipped under the surface.

The guards heard all of the commotion and were closing in. My saviors scrambled back through the fence just as the guards arrived. To this day, I have no idea who saved me. Fearing I was trying to escape, they started to beat me with their rifle butts. I covered my head and tried to protect myself. As I lay there covered in shit, I lost control of my bowels.

That was it, I thought. I was done. But giving up meant death. I had lived with death every day since coming to Korea. The battlefield was like a movie in fast forward. There was so much going on and I couldn't dwell on death very long. Call for the medic, possibly hold the wounded man in my arms, or say a word or two as he passed from life to death.

It was different as a prisoner. I had no way of defending myself other than using my mind and what physical capabilities I could muster. I realized my mind had to be my strength.

For a split second, all of the pain and suffering could have ended.

"No!" my mind screamed.

I couldn't give up. I'd come this far and in that second I set my mind to doing something no one had done. I was going to come back from the morgue. As the Chinese soldiers landed blow after blow on my back and legs, I banished death from my mind. Never again did it enter into it.

The guards finally stopping hitting me and called over two more guards, who threw two buckets of water on me. The two buckets of water didn't do much to clean me up. Then the guards dragged me by my arms back to the morgue.

When they threw me in, it was a repeat performance. First the smell and then the kicks and protests of the other sick and injured. It didn't last long, since I now fit in perfectly and I no longer gave a damn. Once I carved out my spot, I tried to clean up. The shit was caked on and I tried to scrape it off my skin or shake it off my pants. This was my new home, at least until I could figure out how to get out.

It was not long and I was one of the longest residents of this stinking hellhole. As fast as the men died, new individuals were thrown into the room. We were dying thirty and forty a day. Most men just waited until their number was called. I was eating with, sleeping with, talking to living corpses and could do nothing about their dying except to comfort them and show them a little compassion. King seemed to hang on and I believed he would make it.

After a while, I made it around the room and set up next to him. He was a massive black man with a barrel chest and thick arms. I learned that he was a boxer. He'd been the heavyweight boxing champ for the Army in Europe and later the all-Army champion. King had pneumonia.

King had done his best to keep the men in the room in order. His size and booming voice alone commanded respect, and he was healthier than the other dying guys. As I got better, I was able to assist him in keeping as much order as possible considering the situation we were in. First we tried to clean up the room, but getting water was hard. As hard as it was, we no longer let soldiers defecate on themselves and helped those that could make it to the latrine. Overall, we tried to keep the mood up, and new prisoners were no longer greeted by insults and kicks.

I had no idea what was going on outside of the morgue. I still couldn't stand or walk. I dragged myself outside and around to the back of the building, where I could sit against the wall in the sun. It's amazing how the sun warms you no matter how cold it is. It seemed to go right through my body and warm me inside. One day, while I was trying to get some fresh air, I ran across a prisoner who was voluntarily helping the sick and wounded in two of the other buildings. He sat down to have a smoke and we started to talk about conditions at the camp. I asked about my house and Doyle, Smoak and the others. He didn't know anything about them, but he did tell me stories that shocked me about how men mistreated one another. The strong were picking on the weak, taking clothes and food. He told me how one prisoner had kicked another to death. They weren't fighting, the soldier said; one guy did it just because he could. Two days later, the attacker died too.

Many lost control of their minds and did things that they would never have done under normal circumstances. I didn't know what to say. When I heard stories or saw things where men were mistreating one another, I thought of the first night of captivity, when the Chinese dumped the rice on the ground.

What happens to men when they become prisoners?

Why do they change from helping one another and become totally engrossed in themselves, with a totally selfish outlook on life?

Understand I'm not talking about all men, but many never

come to grips with losing their freedom. They feel abandoned by their country and are no longer with men they trust. In their minds, their personal survival becomes paramount and group survival no longer matters.

"You're a good man," I told him. "I don't know many that would work in this hellhole."

I asked him if he knew Vaillancourt and Roberts. He shook his head yes and looked down at his cigarette.

"I did. They both died a couple of weeks ago," he said.

He flicked his cigarette and smiled weakly at me.

"Got to get back," he said.

I sat there in silence. Roberts and Vaillancourt weren't as close to me as Walsh and Hall, but knowing they were gone still hurt. But not like before. The way the guys were dying, thirty or forty a day, another couple deaths didn't register. Plus in the morgue we were all dying.

Most days I sat outside and watched the road that ran behind the back of the building. Small groups of men would walk by to collect wood for the cookhouses. My legs were feeling a little better, and I yelled to a pair of guys to bring me back some limbs that I could fashion into crutches. The next day they threw me a couple of limbs that were V-shaped on one end. The next day, I tried to cross the road.

Steadying myself on the new crutches, I slid my left foot forward. Pain shot through my body. I paused and caught my breath. Then, slowly, I slid my right foot forward. The pain shot through my back again, but not as sharp. Left. Right. Left. The width of the road was only about fifteen feet, but it took me all day. The pain was excruciating. But the next day, I did it again. I went out and walked the width of the road every day for weeks. One day, one of the guys getting wood stopped and clapped for me.

Soon, my right leg started to straighten up. My left leg was still useless, but by then I was walking down the road toward the river. Again, it took me all day and I covered less than one hundred yards. When I got to the bottom, some English prisoners carried me back up the hill. I did this every day until I walked back up the hill alone. The weather was getting warmer and my left leg started to heal. I wanted to be ready for the summer. That is when I had the best chance to escape.

When the ice on the river finally thawed, the Chinese started letting the prisoners wash in the river. Some of the guys offered to carry me down and help me get into the water. It was freezing cold, but believe it or not it felt great. It was the first time I was able to clean myself since the night in the trench. I washed my clothes and body. It was wonderful. The bath and cleaning of my clothes really invigorated me. For days afterward, I went at walking with much more energy. Every day my legs improved, to the point where I could walk without the jerry-rigged crutches. Within two weeks, I barely used them at all.

Soon, the Chinese were back. This time, they came to tell

me I was leaving the morgue. I couldn't believe it. But as it sank in, I thought about King. Of all the people there, I wished that he would heal enough to get out. I was sad that I would more than likely never know who the two guys were that saved me from drowning in the slit trench.

"King, get off your ass and get out of here," I said as the guards escorted me out.

"Good luck, Rich," he said.

I never thought I'd ever see King again. But four years later,

Slowly and painfully, my legs begin to straighten.
Sketch by author

I was in a jeep at Fort Dix, New Jersey, when I saw him directing traffic. He was a military police officer.

"Pull over," I told the driver and hopped out as soon as he stopped.

Walking into the intersection, I called out King's name.

"Rich?" King said.

King and I had a reunion right in the middle of the intersection as cars looked on. Both of us had actually made it.

But the better reunion was back in the prison camp. As the Chinese marched me down the hill, I had no idea where they were taking me. I was surprised when they brought me back to my old house. When the guards shoved me through the door, Doyle and Smoak couldn't believe their eyes.

"Welcome back," Doyle said.

Since no one had ever come back from the morgue, the guys peppered me with questions about my treatment.

"What treatment?" I said and they all laughed.

I told them we never received any medicine. Got less food and the room smelled like a cesspool. I told how I'd almost drowned in the trench and that two guys from the black compound saved my life.

"It was a shitty situation," I said, and again they all laughed.

It felt good to be back with my guys. No one came back from the morgue, so being the first one meant something. For me it was better than medicine. My morale was sky high. I had made it and now set my sights on escaping.

CHAPTER NINETEEN

TRUMAN'S RUNNING DOGS

Since I'd been in the morgue , the Chinese had started putting a lot of pressure on us. We were required to spend hours in lectures and discussion groups supervised by Chinese political officers. The program focused on what was wrong with the United States. Everything was corrupt, from our government, to our economic structure, educational system and press.

Much of their emphasis was on lower class laborers in the United States and how they were exploited by our government.

"It was not our fault we attacked North Korea, it was our corrupt government," Doyle told me, repeating the day's lesson. "The Chinese are peace-loving people and mean us no harm."

My God, where had I heard all of this before? It was the same crap that officer had told me during my first interrogation.

The day after I returned from the morgue, Doyle took me aside. I had a lot of catching up to do.

"Guards came at all hours to escort prisoners to the camp's headquarters," Doyle said.

"What for?" I asked. "We don't have much intelligence value. I have no idea what is going on in the war."

"They want to discuss what we heard in the lecture earlier," Doyle said. "They also have us learning Chinese songs. But we've changed a few lines. One ends with 'Who flung dung at Mao Tse Tung?'"

Doyle explained that the political officers began by breaking you down physically so you started to agree with them just to get them off your back. When this happened, they would be on you full-force pushing you to make a statement against the United States government or to make a statement as to the wonderful treatment you were receiving. Next, you'd be one of the turncoats up on stage leading a lecture. Listening to Doyle, I was determined to fight them at every turn. There was no way I was going to allow myself to be hijacked by their group thinking or be a puppet of their oppressive government.

The Chinese had also started to clean up the camp since I'd been gone, in hopes of winning us over. Any man sick or dying was taken to the "hospital" and kept out of sight. We were still dying in great numbers; it had just been removed from our sight. They also tried to improve our diet. Prisoners even started to make steam bread by taking balls of dough and placing them on a bamboo rack over a pot of steaming water.

"I will leave a hundred men to die to save one progressive," the base commander reportedly said.

I wasn't back a day before I followed the rest of the house to my first lecture.

Before I went to the morgue they were hammering away on the theme that the United States was the aggressor and had orchestrated the attack on North Korea. Following it up by showing our imperialistic transgressions around the world. They tried to substantiate this by showing all the countries where we had United States troops stationed or naval forces controlling sea lanes around the world.

Today's lecture was directed toward tearing down our capitalistic system and showing how the captains of industry controlled the money and suppressed the masses. Supposedly in the socialistic system the masses would share equally in the state-run economy. The state would control every facet of life and provide for everyone from cradle to grave. A Utopia where everyone would share equally. In their convoluted way of thinking this would lead us to the conclusion that socialism/communism would benefit all mankind. I believe this was not really intended to produce turncoats for anything more than propaganda; however, I think they hoped that some of the returning POWs would believe enough that they would spread the seeds of doctrine when they returned to their country. This was a tough sell to the group I was in. We outwardly challenged the loss of individual freedom under their system. The Chinese became quite agitated.

The Chinese were constantly trying to develop individuals to reinforce their philosophy. They would entice them with better medical care, food and, in general, treating them as friends.

The lectures were followed by discussion groups on the content of the lecture. In our room it was a joke.

However, it was no joke to the Chinese. We were repeatedly being taken to the Chinese headquarters and questioned about the lecture and why we were not cooperating in our room discussions. I became one of their prime targets. I was taken to the headquarters on numerous occasions. It was always the same thing. Attempts to reeducate me, which always broke down, then threats and promises that things would get better once I cooperated.

"Why do you not cooperate? Other men do," the political officer would ask.

The Chinese had a small group of American and British prisoners who helped with lectures, wrote propaganda and even taped anti-American broadcasts. In return, they were being fed better than the rest of the prisoners. One or two were seen coming and going outside the camp without guards. I learned early on not to accuse someone of being an informer or collaborator based on rumors. The Chinese were smart and made it look as though an individual was cooperating, hoping that rejection by the other prisoners would force him to seek comfort.

When I was called to a session with an interrogator, I always made myself believe I had one or two of my roommates with me. If I said anything, I first thought what would Doyle think if he could hear me. Most times I just kept silent. I'd learned that outwitting the interrogator was impossible. The less I said, the better. I just looked at them with a blank stare. I was getting very good at detaching myself from the conversation. I knew that they would like to kill me, but they needed to be careful not to destroy their so-called lenient policy without a damned good explanation or lie.

We all tried to resist, even if it only meant not paying attention. One night the Chinese had been going at a large group of us and it was getting close to morning. Lectures followed by discussion all designed to keep us up—they hoped our sleep-deprived minds would give in to their demands.

Finally, one of the men in the group stood up and started singing "God Bless America." Before the Chinese realized what was happening, we were all on our feet singing. The Chinese let us finish, but we knew a punishment was coming.

A few days later, the guards surrounded our buildings. They formed us up in a column of threes and moved us to the road that ran down the valley to the river. The first platoon of which I was a part consisted of about sixty prisoners. With the two other platoons, we totaled about 150 men. The rest of the men in the camp lined up along the road. An English-speaking Chinese officer announced over the loudspeaker that we were being moved to a work camp.

"Truman's running dogs and Wall Street warmongers are disrupting your peaceful chances for education," the officer said, his thickly accented English booming from the speakers.

We were all scared. This had never happened before. But we walked down the road with our heads held high and smiling. As they marched us onto two barges at the dock, the Chinese guards also told the other prisoners that we were to be worked to death and they would never see us again. The Chinese were in such a hurry to get rid of us that one of the barges we were loaded on tore down an electric wire as it pulled away from the dock.

The farther we got from shore, the more nervous I got. Standing at the rail and looking into the dark, cold, swirling water, I worried that these bastards were going to get us in the deep water and pull the plug and sink the barges. We were in no condition to swim very far.

We sailed a few miles down the river. I kept my eyes fixed on the shore, hoping to be back on land soon. Finally, the Chinese guards unloaded us at a pier and marched us north to a clearing on the backwater of the Yalu River. The North Koreans were going to build long houses by the bank, and we spent the next few days carrying lumber down from the hills. We had to walk three or four miles to the hills where we were cutting the timber. Word was that the six long houses were being built to house more prisoners. The work was hard, but it beat sitting through the lectures.

The next day, we were taken back to the dock, where we started to unload the supply barges. We were unloading burlap bags full of grain. It took two of us side by side to carry one sack. We'd periodically drop a sack in the water. But the Chinese caught on and made us fish the sacks out of the water. They became our rations. The Chinese had a scale by the docks, and some of us got a chance to weigh ourselves. I weighed a grand total of 108 pounds.

We continued to sabotage the Chinese effort when we could. At the bottom of the hill there were telephone lines running along the side of the road. As we carried the wood down the hill to the work site, we'd drop a log against the line, snapping it. Each time, Chinese repairmen would walk up the road and splice it back together. After we did this a few times, we decided that we should take out a huge piece of the line. Using two logs, we knocked down a large section of the wire farther up the hill and hid the broken wire. We could always find a use for it. When the repairmen found the problem, they had no wire with them. What was normally a six-mile hike turned into twelve that day.

A couple of the guys picked up some good lighters with plenty of pinesap in them. As we walked along the road, we set the thatched roofs of the Chinese houses on fire. By the time the houses started burning, we were well down the road. We burned three houses before the Chinese became suspicious.

Despite working many hours building the long houses, we were still required to attend lectures. And once a Chinese acting troupe came to town. It was their version of a USO show, called *The White-Haired Girl.*

The story line was simple. A peasant family could not pay the taxes demanded by the dastardly landowner. So he takes the peasant's beautiful young black-haired daughter as his concubine. She suffers terribly under his demented demands but eventually escapes to the mountains. Years later as the People's Liberation Army frees the people, the girl returns to the village. But now her hair has turned completely white.

The play was well done, and the Chinese officers and soldiers hung on every word. They saw the girl's story as their own. They clapped when the People's Liberation Army arrived. The play, of course, omitted the fact that Mao killed thousands of people in his drive to take control of China. We laughed and cheered when the landlord dragged the young girl away. The Chinese guards were not amused, and for days after there was an awkward silence.

Later, the Chinese political officers held a lecture on the American Civil War. We paid no attention to the Chinese lecturers, and fifty-eight years later I still don't remember much of what was said. After the presentation, the political officer passed out questions dealing with the lecture. It had always been my policy not to write anything on these papers; however, on this particular one I wrote one sentence: "The war was fought to preserve the Union."

The next day, the political officer started the lecture with a reward ceremony. The officer read off a few soldiers' names and gave each one a packet of tobacco. Mine was the first on the list. To say I was shocked is an understatement. I looked around at Doyle and Smoak.

"This is bullshit," I said.

I basically believed that most of the men in our camp at this time would not collaborate with the Chinese. However, prudence called for confidence in a very small number. My circle became very tight. I only shared my thoughts and plans with Doyle and Smoak. We tried to keep a low profile, thereby giving us a better chance of being successful in coming up with an escape plan or sabotage.

"Get the goddamn tobacco, Rich," Doyle said.

I was completely dumbfounded as I stepped up and took my pack of tobacco and sat back down to a chorus of boos. On the return trip to our house, some of the other prisoners started to yell at me. They called me a collaborator and a traitor. They might as well have beaten me to a pulp. It wouldn't have hurt as much. Some of the others stuck up for me. Lucky for me the majority of the men knew me well enough that there was not a doubt in their minds that the Chinese were attempting to destroy my influence. I knew what would follow: numerous visits to the headquarters. The bastards had set me up and would now try for the kill.

That afternoon, the guards came to take me up to the head-quarters. I walked into the room, which was sparsely decorated with a single table. Sitting behind the table were three of the Chinese political lecturers. As soon as I sat down, they started on me. One told me how I had listened and showed that I was willing to learn. They waited for me to answer.

"I never believe any of the fucking lies you bastards are put-ting out," I said.

Nothing I could have said would have had the same impact on them as using curse words. They hated it.

"You do not speak to us this way," one of them said.

"Fuck you, you sons of bitches."

Their faces were flushed. One of them headed toward me like he was going to hit me, but he pulled up short. I tried to stare them all down. I had hoped they would beat me or throw me in the hole. However, in my mind I knew that they would not do this because they would only waste this attempt to un-dermine my influence on the rest of the men.

"Why you speak this way? You will be sorry."

My heart was pumping a mile a minute. I didn't say another

word. After hours of questions, they finally let me go and walked me back to my room. When I got there, I told Doyle and Smoak what had taken place. Smoak looked at me in disbelief.

"Jesus Christ, Rich, have you lost your mind?"

Doyle was mad.

"What the hell were you thinking?" he said. "They are going to be watching us like hawks. Look, we know what got to you, but you need to promise us that you will calm down."

I looked at them sheepishly and promised that I would get myself under control.

On my next visit to the headquarters they didn't mince words. They told me in no uncertain terms that if I continued to disrespect them and be outwardly uncooperative, when the war ended I would not be released. I would be held back for five years. This was not the first or last time I would hear this, and I shook it off as one of their idle threats. But unlike before, I didn't assault them with curse words. Instead, I just stared ahead and tried to think of anything but their questions.

When it got warm enough, the Chinese let us stake out a baseball field near the river. We didn't have any balls or bats, but we went through the motions. We made teams and selected umpires. We called balls and strikes. It sounds weird, but we had a lot of fun. We spent hours out there.

Sometimes, we'd stop the game to watch dogfights, since the camp was right under MiG Alley. The Chinese fighters would come across the Manchurian border and American fighters would soon appear. I stood on the bank and watched as the fighters, high above, corkscrewed and banked in their elaborate dance of death. Most times the fights ended in a draw, with the planes flying off out of sight. Sometimes, we'd see a parachute descend. It took an unbelievable amount of time before the pilot disappeared behind the mountain. I have no idea how high they must have been when they bailed out.

Late one afternoon, a lone American fighter jet came screaming down the river. We were out on the ball field. At first, it scared the hell out of us. It went by in a flash but doubled back and flew straight down the river. We could see the pilot looking down, and as he passed, the pilot waved and wiggled his wings at us. There were no words to describe how that incident made us feel. God bless him. He probably never knew what that simple act did for us. It was a very long time before we stopped talking about it. And we'd achieved our goal with the ball field. The Chinese refused to identify POW camps, but the ball field did the trick.

A company of prisoners was brought in from Camp 5 near Pyoktong that fall. Just before their arrival we were told that peace talks had begun in July of 1951. Coinciding with this we were given a Chinese newspaper printed in English. It was full of Communist propaganda, including how the North Koreans were bending over backward to accommodate all the ridiculous demands made by the United Nations delegation. Despite the outlandish bickering, the peace talks were moving forward only because of the tireless efforts of the North Korean delegation.

The new prisoners brought information that the peace talks had terminated due to the U.N. forces' violation of the Panmunjom restricted area, a no-man's-land along the 38th parallel that separated the countries. Whatever this was about, we were sure we would soon be told how the UN forces deliberately undermined the talks. The new prisoners also told us that the Chinese had formalized courses of instruction to the point that the prisoners were now calling Camp 5 "The University of Pyoktong." Like us, this new batch of prisoners had become a disruptive force. So the Chinese shipped them down to our camp.

We finished the buildings that fall and were surprised when the Chinese let us move in. The buildings were sixty feet long and sixteen feet wide. Thirty of us were sleeping on each side of the buildings, with a four-foot aisle running from one end to the other. Each end had a single door. When it got cold, the Chinese issued us a winter-padded jacket, pants and hat similar to the Chinese uniform. They also set up a potbellied stove in each dorm. It did little to heat the building, but psychologically it did wonders. Soon after winter set in, I got sick. I started running a high fever and was coughing up green and yellow mucus. Doyle and Smoak moved me near the stove and kept me hydrated with hot water. A medic told me I had pneumonia. I thought of Graves and was grateful that I wasn't still in the morgue. After a couple of days, the fever broke and I got better. Doyle and Smoak both said they were sure I'd make it.

"Yeah, Rich, some of us thought we might need to dip you in the shithouse again to make you better," Smoak said.

Every night a Chinese officer would enter the building at one end, walk down the aisle with a flashlight and check to see if everyone was present.

We'd stolen a rope, and one night we rigged up one of the guys by putting the rope under his shirt so that he could be suspended from the exposed roof beam. We tied a hangman's noose and slipped it around his neck. Then we waited. We heard the dirt crunch under his boots as the Chinese officer approached the door and stepped into the building. A thin beam of light from his flashlight cut through the darkness. It swept back and forth across the room, pausing for a second on each bed.

The officer got a quarter of the way down before his flashlight shined on the feet of the hanging man.

The Chinese guard stopped immediately and took a deep breath. The light moved quickly up the hanging man, finally stopping on his face, head cocked to one side, tongue hanging out. The officer dropped the light and we could hear him dash for the door. Two minutes later, ten guards arrived. They were all trying to squeeze in the doorway. All of them were talking at once. In the lead was the officer, who was pointing where he'd found the man hanging. But when he got back, there was no body. There was no rope. And there was no flashlight. All gone, never to be seen again. The Chinese were raising hell and we were all lying there snickering. Finally, they stomped out, the officer protesting and still pointing to where the body was.

We all laughed ourselves to sleep.

CHAPTER TWENTY

PREPARATION FOR ESCAPE

In early spring, my legs were finally in shape to begin thinking about escape again.

Every day, I stared at the river. It was the best way out. I figured we could lash a few logs together and two or three of us could float to freedom. If we stayed low in the water, it would be impossible to see us. We'd look like some debris going down the river. The plan was to travel at night and spend days under cover on the bank. We still didn't know the backwaters of the river, but we didn't know the mountains either. So overland was a problem too. Plus, going by water would be easier on my legs.

During the next few weeks I started looking for logs at least four feet long. I found two and stashed them down by the river.

I also started hunting around for the telephone wire we'd stolen. It would be perfect to lash the logs together. I started to ask around, trying to see who had it. But I had to be careful. There was no doubt in my mind that the Chinese had informers. How many and who they were was anybody's guess. They very possibly had someone in each room. As much as I would have liked to think there was no one in my room, it was possible.

I also needed a partner. It would be too hard alone. The old two-man foxhole certainly was true in this case. I trusted Doyle, but the winter had taken a lot out of him. I didn't think he could make it. Smoak could be trusted and he was tough. There was no doubt he could make it. One afternoon, I pulled him aside. He followed me outside the house and we walked close to the river.

"That is our way out," I told Smoak when we'd gotten to the bank.

He nodded and smiled.

"I've got two logs down there ready. All we need to do is lash them up and float out of here," I said. "We travel at night and hide during the day."

Smoak liked the plan. We made a decision to move west during the night then leave the river and move southeast for two days, then move east to the coast. But like me, he wondered if we needed another guy.

"If something happened to one man, two of us could possibly help take him along," I said.

"Right, but if one of us can't continue, the others should go on," Smoak said.

He looked at my leg. "You think you can do it with those legs?"

"I'll be fine," I said. "I can make it. My legs feel better. Stronger every day."

"So who is our third guy?" Smoak asked.

I suggested Gonzalez. He was a smart, tough Latino. He and I had talked many times on detail getting firewood or carrying timber down from the mountain. From Texas, he had broad shoulders and a thick head of black hair. Of average build, he was strong and always did more than his share of the work. More than once, we talked about escaping. No details or plans. We were too careful for that. But his desire to get out matched ours. Smoak wanted to take a couple of days to see what he could find out about Gonzalez.

A few days later, the team was set. Gonzalez had passed muster, and Smoak and I set out to test the logs. Just after midnight, we walked to the latrine and stripped. Bundling our clothes in a ball, we snuck down to the bank and slid the logs from their hiding place in a clump of bushes and into the water. The river was cold and sent a shiver through my body as we waded deep into the water, our clothes balanced in the center of the raft. Clinging to the logs on either side, we paddled and kicked our way across the river to the far bank and then doubled back to the camp. The logs worked perfectly, and three hours later we were back in our building. No one knew. The next morning, over our breakfast of maize, we told Gonzalez how easy it had been to get the logs into the water. This was going to work.

"Now all we need is warmer weather," I said. "I froze my ass off."

Gonzalez laughed, but Smoak just grunted.

"I don't feel well," he said. "My stomach is killing me."

Soon, Smoak was doubled over. Doyle tried to get the Chinese to do something, but they ignored his pleas. Soon Smoak couldn't talk. He just lay in bed and moaned. When the pain got really bad, he screamed. Finally, he passed out. His face was locked in a tortured grimace and his skin had turned ashen. At noon, the medic that was helping him turned to us and shook his head.

"He's dead."

The words landed on us like mortar rounds. I just stood there staring at his face in shock. Dead? How could this have happened in such a short time? Only seven months ago men were dying all around us. It was normal. Since we'd moved, prisoners didn't die anymore. We were the survivors. This wasn't supposed to happen anymore. The shock quickly boiled up into a rage. There was talk of marching against the Chinese headquarters and making demands. For what, I wasn't sure.

"Rich, we need to show the Chinese in the strongest way

we can that we demand medical care when someone is sick," Doyle said.

I followed the group out of the room and up the hill to the headquarters. We were screaming at the top of our lungs, demanding that the officers come out and talk with us. Guards blocked our way. Prisoners in other buildings stood outside and watched. They had astonished looks on their faces. We were out of our minds with rage. We were standing on a mound just high enough that we were looking down at the guards. The Chinese were nervous. The camp commander and three or four of the political officers approached us slowly.

"Get back to your building," one of the English-speaking political officers said.

We shouted him down.

"Get back," the commander said, "and I will talk to your leaders. But only if you go back to your building."

We went back to the building and for a while thought we'd shocked the Chinese into changing things. But nothing changed. We never saw any doctors or medicine. We all fell into a funk. I could still hear Smoak's humming and infectious laugh. Gonzalez and I were stuck looking at the river, knowing we knew how to get out. But we no longer had a third man.

The river still ended up being our way out. About a month later, the Chinese marched our building out of the camp and onto a barge moored at the pier. We had no idea why the guards were moving us, but it was pretty clear that our protest hadn't helped things. The Chinese felt it was better to move the troublemakers.

The new camp was built near a village. It was surrounded on three sides by open fields. As we walked through the village, a large double gate loomed before us. The security at the camp was the best we'd seen. The gate was flanked by two guard posts. A tall barbed wire fence with guard towers at fifty-yard intervals ringed the camp.

Inside the wire, the guards marched us to mud huts. There were only ten to twelve small buildings in the camp. One was a cookhouse. The first thing I did was volunteer for a detail to find firewood. It allowed me to get out of the camp and check out the area. Along the way, I saw a small schoolhouse with a map on the wall. On our way back to camp the Chinese guards were in their normal lackadaisical mode. Positioned at the front and back of the column, they were too far away to see all of us. I moved up to the front, and when we got adjacent to the school building I dropped my wood bundle and shot into the building. I ripped the map off the wall and stuffed it into my shirt. I dashed out, picked up my bundle of wood and kept walking. My heart was in my throat.

"What the hell are you doing, Rich?" one of the guys asked.

"I just wanted to see what was in the building," I said.

"What the hell did you expect to find in there? A good-looking Korean teacher."

"You never know," I answered. I could feel the thick paper of the map under my shirt.

I could hardly wait to show Gonzalez the map. Later that night, I got him to the side and told him about it.

"Jesus Christ, Rich, are you crazy? They would have ripped you a new ass if they had caught you," he said.

"But they didn't catch me," I said.

We spread the map out, but it was a little disappointing. Not much detail. However, it showed the coast and the river. It was more than we'd ever had before. I told Gonzalez I was working in the cookhouse and would start stashing food. My job was to carry water from the well outside the gate to the cookhouse. Every day, I balanced two five-gallon cans of water on the ends of a chogie stick. A guard came with me as I shuffled along like the Koreans. The guards didn't follow me all the way to the well. Instead, they hung by the road, just keeping me and the well in sight.

Unlike at past camps, civilians still lived in the village. When the guards weren't looking, I would bow and wave to them. They looked Japanese, probably leftovers from the long and brutal occupation during World War II, and they seemed intimidated by the Chinese. One day, I interrupted a young girl getting water at the well. She and her family lived at a nearby house. When she'd seen me before, the girl had run off and watched me from inside the house.

This day, I filled my two five-gallon containers and noticed an empty jug sitting nearby. I dropped the bucket into the well, pulled it up and filled her jug. After a few days of watching me get water, the girl wasn't afraid. I filled her bucket and smiled. My hope was to build enough rapport that when Gonzalez and I made our dash, the civilians would help. Worst case, they wouldn't tell.

One day, a middle-aged Korean man was standing near the well. He was small, with thick black hair and dark eyes. When he saw me looking at him, he bowed and pointed to his wrist like he wanted a wristwatch.

I nodded my head yes and he turned and walked away. That night, I told Gonzalez about the Korean.

"I am sure he wants a watch," I said. "Maybe if we get him one, he'll help us escape."

Neither one of us knew of anyone offhand who still had a watch. But we hoped that we could get one. If we could get the Korean to take us part of the distance, it would make our chances that much better. The one thing that kept nagging in the back of my mind was that the Korean could be setting us up. Once we got out, he could have us killed or, after he got what he wanted, turn us in to the North Korean Police.

"See how far you can take him," Gonzalez said.

Our plan had changed since we moved. Since I got the map, we'd decided to skip the river. Instead, our plan was to move to the west coast, look for a boat and take our chances on being picked up by our Navy. We figured it was seventy miles as the crow flies to the coast.

We needed to time our escape so that it was dark. We had the moon cycle and guard posts diagrammed on the reverse side of the map and waited for a dark night to run. We didn't see any real problem getting through the fences. It was easy to wiggle through the gaps in the wire. Now all we had to do was get the Korean on our side and wait for the moon cycle.

The Korean wasn't there the next day, but he showed up again at the well the following day. I made sure the guard wasn't looking and pointed to my wrist. He nodded his head yes. Then I pointed at myself and him and mimed us walking away with my fingers. He kept shaking his head yes. I did it again just to make sure he understood. All of a sudden the guard started shouting and waving at me to hurry up. I waved to the man and hurried back to the road.

When I got back to the camp, I found out that the Chinese guards had taken Gonzalez to headquarters for questioning. This wasn't unusual, and I figured he'd be back later that night. These sessions usually took thirty minutes, or until they got tired of hearing themselves talk. After about an hour, the kitchen crew and I watched as guards marched Gonzalez to a hole near the center of the camp. After a slight shove, Gonzalez climbed inside and the guard stood near the entrance.

This looked serious. Had someone told the Chinese about

our escape plan? I was the one who'd stolen the map. I was the one trying to make a deal with the Korean. It made no sense that the Chinese had Gonzalez in the hole. He must have said something to someone. That night I moved the map from the hole near my house to another hole a little farther away.

The next day, Gonzalez was still in his hole. But the guards came by the cookhouse to get him some food. I took a bowl and stuck in it a note I'd scrawled on some loose paper in the kitchen: "Hang in there."

After I did it, I thought that was not too smart. If the Chinese found it, it would cause Gonzalez more trouble and the whole kitchen crew would be in trouble. The Chinese never discovered it, and I hoped that it gave Gonzalez a boost down at the bottom of the hole.

In the middle of all of this, my Korean villager disappeared. A day or two later someone was telling a story about the Chinese taking a Korean away with his hands tied behind his back. I had no way of knowing if it was my man, but I never saw him again.

With Gonzalez in the hole and no help from the outside, my escape plan was temporarily destroyed.

CHAPTER TWENTY-ONE

THE LAST YEAR

"Get up! Get up!"

The Chinese guards burst into our huts shouting and pulling us onto our feet.

"Bring your belongings and get outside!"

Half-asleep, I collected up my padded jacket, blanket and towel and staggered with the rest outside. Old American Army trucks were lined up by the gate. Their engines rumbled as the guards shoved us toward the open tailgates. As we walked, I could feel the map scraping my legs. I'd stuffed it into my pants when the guards weren't looking.

We'd only been at this camp for eighteen days. Now we were on the move again. Just before the guards threw open the gate, we saw Gonzalez. They had taken him out of the hole to his room to gather his belongings. The guards were marching him to the back of our truck. I was happy to see him.

"I'm fine, guys. Just fine," he said as we helped him aboard.

"Why did they put you in the hole?" I asked.

"I don't know," he said, settling into a seat next to me. "They kept asking me general questions about everyone."

I wanted to ask him if they knew about the escape. Did they know we had a map? But I couldn't in front of the others. We headed east for hours. The only thing that stood out was we passed what I thought were a couple of mines, one small steel mill and a train engine repair shop, all located within a mile of one another. In the excitement of the move, at first it didn't cross my mind that we were traveling in broad daylight.

Doyle noticed my nervousness.

"What's up?"

"Christ, do you realize that we are moving in the daylight?"

Doyle just looked at me and grimaced. We never mentioned it again.

We were on a straight stretch of road heading east, when a truck going west passed us. In the back of the truck there were two Catholic nuns and one civilian Caucasian male. They were standing and waving to us, and in a second they were gone. We had heard rumors of Catholic nuns being held by the Chinese. We all thought that the male might have been Frank Knowles, the photographer who was being held in the officers' camp. It was amazing the uplifting feeling it gave all of us just seeing the three of them. They dominated the conversation for many miles. Who were they? Where were they going? If this was Knowles, where was he coming from? Twenty questions, none of which could be answered.

The trucks finally rolled to a stop in front of a schoolhouse. A tall fence surrounded it. Each truck unloaded and we were corralled into the fenced yard. Guards patrolled outside the wire. Doyle figured we were close to Mampo, a large city with a railhead.

Inside the yard, they split us into groups by rooms. They made us strip and searched us two at a time. While the first pair got dressed, the next pair stripped. I still had the map. The bucket that we got our food in was sitting by my leg. I looked straight at one of the guys that had finished dressing. It was O'Keefe. I looked at him and then down at the bucket. At the same time, I palmed the map and slipped it out of my pants. Holding it against my leg, I dropped it into the bucket. O'Keefe stepped over and picked the bucket up. I turned and started to take my clothes off just as the Chinese turned to me. O'Keefe walked out of the yard. My heart was beating so hard I could hardly breathe.

After the search, they loaded us on the trucks and moved us across a bridge over a large stream. O'Keefe handed me the map and I put it back into my pants.

"That was close," I said to O'Keefe. "Thanks for the help."

We pulled up to a gate, with seven or more buildings spread

out in the fenced-in area. We were put in an old school building. A hall ran down the middle of the building. Four rooms that I guess at one time had been classrooms became our bedrooms. Sixty of us were put into two rooms. The rooms had wooden sleeping platforms running around the perimeter, two feet off the floor. The best thing was the presence of a potbellied stove. We could look forward to a little heat during the winter.

There was an outside latrine at one end of the building. It soon began to stink, since more than one hundred people used it on a daily basis. The odor was awful. For me, it was like old times in the morgue.

As usual, I wandered around the camp talking to some of the others. There were British, Turkish and some American prisoners in the compound right next to where we were. I started looking for guys from Philadelphia or close by in Pennsylvania. I soon found Charles Wray and three others from Pennsylvania.

We were all together one day shooting the bull when Wray fished out a picture.

"Hey, I have a picture of my girlfriend."

Of course everybody wanted to see it, so he passed it around. It got to me and I noticed that this was only half of a picture. I looked at it closely and then started to laugh.

"Do you know who is on the other part of the photo?" They all looked at me. "I know who's on the other part. Me."

"Bullshit, Rich, who are you shitting?" Wray said.

"I'm telling you, it's me. That girl is Claire, my father's girlfriend's daughter," I said. Wray's eyes had grown wide and his mouth hung open, stunned. "We took that picture in June of 1950 when I visited her home with my father."

That blew everybody's mind. Unbelievable. I stared at the picture for a while longer. I could still remember the exact moment. For the first time in a while, I thought of home and my family. I hoped that my father was happy. Did they know I was alive? I never received any mail and didn't know if anyone had received the two Mother's Day cards that I had made and was able to send. I hoped they knew I was alive.

The Chinese left us alone for a couple of weeks, and we all settled into a routine of cleaning, cooking and sleeping. Then all of a sudden the Chinese started giving us lectures on germ warfare. This was part of the great re-education system. The majority of the population was uneducated, so for the most part they did not have to be re-educated, they only had to be educated through the words of their great leader Mao Tse-tung. This type of education required constant reinforcement. They pounded away with the same garbage, over and over again.

Our planes dropped chafe, thousands of small pieces of aluminum foil that blocked out enemy radar. The Communists had convinced their soldiers and the North Korean civilians that this was a form of germ warfare. They had everyone wearing masks and carrying jars with tweezers or chopsticks so that they could pick up the small pieces of foil. There was no better example of Communist control of the masses.

The winter of 1952–53 was livable compared to the past two winters. We were allowed to select our own leaders and organize committees to work on different facets of our daily life. A sanitation committee, athletic committee, a daily action committee—all brought some semblance of order to our lives. Food had improved too. We got steamed bread, vegetables and rice; once in a while some fish and meat, but it was usually just a scrap. The change in diet was enough to let us gain some weight.

We were also receiving English newspapers from Communist countries, including the New York *Daily Worker*. Printed by the Communist Party of the United States, it was a propaganda rag, but it had a small entertainment and sports section that we looked forward to reading. I got ahold of a copy of *The Last Frontier* by Howard Fast. The book tells the story of the Cheyenne Indians in the 1870s and their bitter struggle to flee Oklahoma. I also read *Spartacus*, about the leader of a Roman slave revolt.

Fast was branded a Communist in 1947, which is why the Chinese gave us the books. But I didn't care, for me it was an escape. The stories not only took me away from the prison camp, but showed that suffering is part of the human experience and it can be overcome. A good lesson and one that I'd learned through experience.

In the spring, all types of athletic equipment began to arrive as well. We formed teams and started to have soccer, football, volleyball and basketball tournaments. We should have known that the sudden interest by the Chinese in athletics and competition was more than just concern for our well-being. It was all in preparation for their great "Peace Olympics" to be held in Pyoktong.

The Olympics were part of the Chinese propaganda machine showing how wonderfully they treated U.N. prisoners. It was fifty years before I realized how the men who participated were exploited. When my mother died, my sister found an unopened envelope from London containing a large magazine full of stories from the camps. It included a large section on the "Peace Olympics" held at Pyoktong. The entire magazine was enough to make me sick.

The track and field events were highlights for me. To the surprise of everyone, I won the preliminary hundred- and two-hundred-meter runs. My legs had gained that much strength.

"You know, Rich," Doyle said. "You win and you'll go to the Olympics."

I was on my way to the makeshift track to race in the final heat. I didn't want to be part of their Olympics.

"So I guess I am going to lose."

I got to the starting line and waited for the signal to go. I'd never thrown a race or game, and I was having trouble doing it. I knew I had to lose, but I shot out of the starting blocks.

My mind knew I had to slow down, but my legs didn't want to lose. Lucky for me, a guy from another company was faster. I came in second place.

I had thought about escape every day, but now escape crossed my mind less and less. Life had become more bearable. We read about peace talks, and in March, the Chinese finally accepted a U.N. proposal to exchange sick and wounded prisoners.

Five months after the exchange, the war was over. The war had begun three years before with a North Korean invasion of South Korea. It ended July 27, 1953, with neither side winning a decisive military victory.

The Chinese had us all in a formation when they announced that a peace agreement had been reached. We stood silently, looking at one another. No one said anything. This news had been a long time coming.

I just stood there, a smile plastered across my face. I looked down at my rail-thin frame. Like a map, it showed my journey. Scars on my back from shrapnel. A missing tooth from the corn. Night blindness from a lack of vitamins, which luckily only lasted for a couple of weeks. I was one of the fortunate ones. I'd survived.

CHAPTER TWENTY-TWO

FREEDOM

The day I left the prison camp, my fifth, I thought about a recurring dream I had. I was on a train going to see Rose. She was on a passing train going in the opposite direction. Somehow we never knew we were passing each other.

But in the dream I knew. It always left me sad. I had the dream on my last night at the prison camp, but it was impossible to feel anything but hope that morning. To this day, when I think of our movement south, I get butterflies in my stomach.

We all climbed into the back of old U.S. Army trucks. There was a great deal of nervous talk. God only knew what freedom would hold for each of us. What would our world be like that we were returning to? How were our families? Did they know we were coming home? Did they know we were alive? What was their situation?

They were moving us to the railhead at Mampo. The Chinese gave one of the prisoners a lock and told him to close the gates after the trucks pulled out. After we passed, he snapped the lock shut, closing some of the darkest chapters in my life.

At Mampo we were loaded in railcars that had recently carried cattle. The residue deposited by the cattle still remained on the floor. It didn't bother me. I looked at it as the sweet smell of freedom on the way. A couple of guys started mooing, and almost instantly everyone was mooing and laughing like hell.

Looking through the wooden slats as we moved, I saw the aftermath of our bombing campaign. Railroads, rail stations, bridges all had been totally destroyed and repaired over and over again. We stopped at a railroad station outside of Pyongyang that was completely destroyed. Only the concrete platforms were left.

Our final destination was a tent city near Panmunjom on the 38th parallel. Every afternoon, we sat impatiently waiting for a motorcycle rider to deliver the list of men to be moved that evening. Day after day this took place. Finally Doyle's name was called, and before he left he handed me his little red book that was filled with his poems and quotations. I spent many hours and days reading the poems over and over. I found one about the men he'd lived with. I studied the lines. A few stuck out:

They can identify all the whiskeys by the way they treat
    the throat.
They've been to all places worth the seeing no matter
    how remote.
They know the distance to the stars measured in light years.
They can answer physics problems that would reduce
    Einstein to tears.
I pity these sagacious fools in their self estimated fame,
    for there is ONE wise one here and that one bears
    MY name.

He was the wise one. He'd kept us together and helped me survive. But now I'd become extremely anxious, and thoughts of getting across on my own ran rampant through my brain. I fought the urge. I'd come too far now to risk escaping. The camp had thinned down to only a couple hundred men when the Chinese finally called my name.

We moved by truck to a holding area consisting of five or six buildings with a pagoda in the center of the square. We were fed a good meal of rice and I think egg drop soup; this was great compared to what we had been receiving. After we finished eating, they separated me and another guy and put us in a building by ourselves with a guard outside the door.

What the hell was going on?

I questioned the other guy. We were so distraught that we never learned each other's name.

"What the hell did you do? Have you been in trouble?"

"Yeah, I was accused of trying to escape and disrupting their lectures," he replied. "I guess being a general pain in their ass. What about you?"

"Pretty much the same," I said. "Did they threaten you with being held back?"

He didn't look up and just nodded his head yes. This was going to be a long night.

The next morning, they had all the other men in formation. I could see a white jeep with four men in blue helmets through a large crack in the door. One started reading names off a clipboard. Adrenaline shot through my body as I slammed into the door, knocking it open and hitting the guard.

"Sergeant Richardson, 13250752, turn my name in," I shouted.

The guard pushed me back into the room. My blood pressure must have gone through the roof. I had a pounding headache and I slumped down onto the floor. My friend sat with me and we both looked at each other and never said a word. I could hear the trucks driving away. These little bastards had finally beaten me.

Another group of prisoners arrived that night. The next morning, after they got in formation, a Chinese officer came and took the two of us out of the room and placed us in the formation. He then had a discussion with a member of the International Commission. The names were called. Mine was the last. We boarded the trucks and proceeded to cross Freedom Bridge to Freedom Village.

When we arrived, I didn't wait for them to drop the tailgate, I jumped right out onto the ground. There were two American escorts for each of us. They grabbed me and I thought, holy shit, these guys were big and muscular. I quickly realized they were average guys. I was just a little skinny.

Our first stop was a tent city in a thousand-yard neutral circle in the rice paddies of Panmunjom. We stripped, showered and de-loused. Having put on slippers and pajamas, we were checked by good-looking nurses. We stayed less than an hour before moving to another building to get uniforms and our first meal.

After our meal, we were flown by helicopter to a replacement depot in Inchon. It was my first helicopter flight, and I sat near the door and watched Korea pass in a blur below me. I felt like screaming, singing and dancing, but instead I remained subdued, quiet and happy inside. At Inchon, we got a couple of thousand dollars in back pay. I was shocked to see where they had deducted my laundry from April 1950 in Austria.

Fifty-seven years have passed and I can still remember how great it felt. Like being born again.

Before we boarded the USNT *Brewster*, we got to call home

for the first time. I reached my dad. I could hear the excitement in his voice. He bombarded me with questions.

"Are you all right? When are you coming home?"

I told him I was in good shape. My father told me he and Cathy had gotten married. He was finally happy, and everyone in both families was fine. Then I detected a change in his voice. After a pause, he told me that Rose was married. I could hear in his voice that he was worried about my reaction.

"Don't worry about me, I'll be okay," I said.

There was some kind of calmness inside of me that was difficult to describe. I'd been through so much that just being free and headed home was enough. I cared about Rose, but I understood that she wasn't going to wait. After worrying about living day in and day out, I wondered if anything would bother me in the future.

The voyage back to California on the *Brewster* was great. They served three meals a day. The small things mattered more now than before. We were subjected to daily debriefings, which were more like interrogations, by intelligence officers. Some of the men couldn't believe they were being put through interrogations like they had done something wrong. Personally, it didn't bother me. I was free, being fed well and sleeping like a baby. I was a survivor and had nothing to hide.

My first session was with a young lieutenant whose name just happened to be Robert Richardson. We weren't kin, but we both had a good laugh about our shared last name.

"We're interested more about the actions of other prisoners than you," he said. "Other prisoners will tell us about you."

"Okay," I said. It sounded like the same old bullshit from an interrogator, only this one was wearing a U.S. uniform.

"We've been waiting for your group. You guys were there for a long time and should give us a real clear picture of life in the camps," he said.

"Fire away," I said. For once, in thirty-four months, I had nothing to hide. I don't remember everything we talked about. I was careful about what I said about the others, but otherwise I told Richardson everything he wanted to know.

At one point, he asked me if I'd seen anything unusual on my way south. I told him that I'd seen three pilots at a train station. We were stopped and I slowly made my way toward them. I don't know why, but the whole scene seemed strange. They acknowledged me with their heads and eyes. The naval officer actually waved at me. He pointed north like the Chinese were taking them that way. They were guarded by two armed Chinese officers. One of them waved me off. I didn't advance any farther, I just stood still until one of the Chinese hollered at me and waved me away. The naval officer smiled at me as I turned and walked back to the train.

"We think they are still holding a number of our airmen," Richardson said.

I found out later that they were trying to get the pilots to confess that the U.N. used chemical weapons. At the end of the session, I watched the lieutenant write a comment on my file: "He was very open and cooperative."

For the rest of the voyage, I stayed on the deck. I sucked in the fresh sea air and basked in the warm breeze. Everything I could hear, smell and see was so full of life. As I looked over the rail of the ship, I remembered three years ago looking down at the sea and praying that I would have the strength to lead my men in combat. Now I was returning by myself. I had been born again, a chance to live for tomorrow, to make the most of every day and never look back. I had survived the greatest laboratory of human behavior, one that no education could ever equal.

Weeks later the Golden Gate Bridge jutted out of the fog as the ship pulled into port. A small band played for a crowd as we docked. They bused us from the ship to a USO building where plane tickets were waiting. We were asked not to leave the building, but I didn't want to be cooped up.

We had a few hours before our flight, so I left and walked around the post. My path took me to the post cemetery. It was very quiet and my thoughts were on all of the men and friends that were no longer with me.

Walsh.

Giroux.

Smoak.

I could feel them standing above me. I hoped they were smiling and happy for me because it was my men, my section, that had kept me motivated and alive. I owed my freedom and survival to them. Shortly after my return to the USO building, we were bused to the San Francisco Airfield. A group of us had a few beers and made final toasts to our freedom.

A number of us flew to Chicago, where we changed planes. When the plane left Chicago, I was the only returning prisoner of war aboard. Although there was a plane full of people, I felt very lonely. I was free and on my way home with mixed emotions. I realized that I had just left men that I had lived with twenty-four hours a day for thirty-four months. It was sad that with all the freedom surrounding me there was an empty feeling. There were also the thoughts of the ones who would never return, the ones whose lives had been lost almost before they began.

When we landed in Philadelphia, the stewardess asked us if we would remain seated for just a minute while a special passenger exited the plane. To my surprise that special passenger was me. I walked down the stairs and onto the tarmac. Waiting there were my mother and father. They hugged and kissed me. This time, unlike on the street before the war, I realized that the act of affection between father and son was a wonderful thing. I will never forget the emotion on my father's face as tears welled up in his eyes.

As I stepped away from my father and mother, a beautiful blonde walked up to me.

"You don't remember me, do you?" she asked. I looked her up and down. It was Claire, the girl on the other half of the photograph.

"Yes, I do, but there have been some changes made."

We both laughed as we hugged. She was now my stepsister.

Cathy, Claire's mother, my sisters, brothers and stepbrothers crowded around me; we kissed, hugged and laughed, just like one big happy family.

We went to my mother's house, where some of my old boyhood friends were waiting, as well as some of the neighbors who came by to wish me well. To my great surprise, Bill Heaggley walked into the house. He'd survived the stomach wound and gotten out of the Army.

We looked at each other and hugged, and I realized that the emotions I had been hiding were about to erupt. I quickly took him upstairs. I didn't want anyone to see me crying. I was sure it surprised Heaggley; he only knew me as a very stoic individual. We talked about Walsh and all the men lost at Unsan. For so long, I thought I was the only one left from our group at Fort Devens. Seeing him filled a void that I hadn't even known was there.

We got together a few times after that. I remember trying to talk him into coming back into the Army. He just looked at me and smiled in his quiet way.

M/Sgt. William Richardson, Jr., of 3409 Dillman st., a repatriated prisoner war, is greeted by his mother, Florence, at International Airport. With them is father. Young Richardson was captured by Communists in 'ovember, 1950.

Philadelphia Inquirer, September 22, 1953. My arrival at Philadelphia Airport.

Author's collection

*   *   *

It dawned on me that the public reaction had drastically changed. When we were going to war in 1950, people cheered us at each railroad station. I remember the way it made us feel to be soldiers, proud to be part of a force going off to defend freedom against Communist aggression. Now on our return there were no crowds cheering, only family and close friends.

Photo that appeared in the *Philadelphia Inquirer* on news that I had been freed from Korea. *Author's collection*

Because I was so happy to be given a second chance at life, it took me a while to realize the change. The only thing that bothered me was that all but their loved ones and very close friends forgot the men and women who'd made the ultimate sacrifice.

A few weeks after I got home, I went to visit Graves's mother. I'd gotten letters from families looking for information about their loved ones. I'd tried to nurse Graves, the nineteen-year-old from Philadelphia who'd died of pneumonia that first winter.

Claire and I met Graves's family at his brother's house in the city. He met me at the door and shook my hand.

"Thank you for coming," he said, leading us into the living room.

He introduced us to Mrs. Graves, a small, thin woman who looked older than her years. I could see a deep sadness in her eyes. Over coffee, she asked me about her son. The atmosphere was tense and the questions were probing.

"When did you meet my son?" she asked, her tone skeptical.

"I met him at the first camp," I told her. "It was in a valley near the Yalu. A frigid place."

We talked about the camp and the terrible conditions for a while longer before she asked how he died.

"He wasn't in pain," I told her, trying to ease her sorrow. "He slipped away in his sleep. He had pneumonia and there was no medicine."

The visit was difficult and I was happy to finally leave. But no matter how hard it was for me, I hoped that it brought some closure to the family. A week later, Graves's mother called screaming at me that I didn't deserve to be alive.

"You should be dead," she said. "Not my son."

I was shocked, and my hand shook as I hung up the phone. I am sorry to say that the majority of the cases where I visited the family or answered a letter wound up this way. No one who hadn't been there was ever going to understand the horror I'd witnessed.

While I was absorbing the sounds and sights of freedom, I was beginning to think about my future. I had been given a second chance and I was determined that I was not going to blow it. Claire and I became inseparable and I was falling in love with her. My only fear was that the feeling might not be mutual.

We had a wonderful Christmas holiday and both realized that we were definitely meant to be together. During a New Year's party, I gave Claire an engagement ring. She said yes. We announced to everyone that we were getting married. There were happy people, sad people and mad people. To tell the story behind this statement would take another book. But five children and fifty-six years later, we're still happily married.

Shortly after all of the prisoners returned home, there was a rush to condemn and try men who allegedly collaborated with the enemy.

Murphy, an engineer sergeant, called me. He was being ordered to appear before a board of inquiry to defend himself against statements that he had collaborated with the Chinese. Murphy was a good guy, but to some he was a loudmouth from New York. There were a number of guys who were not used to this big city type and it aggravated the hell out of them. Yes, he had been called to the Chinese headquarters a number of times, but no more than the average guy. He wasn't a collaborator.

"Will you testify on my behalf?" he said, his voice hollow, as if having to defend himself after years of survival was too much.

Without a second thought, I said yes.

"Who in the hell made these statements?" I asked.

But Murphy didn't know. The Army wouldn't release the names of his accusers. It was hard to defend yourself against statements made by unknown individuals. At that time I was a first sergeant of G Company, 364th Infantry Regiment, Fort Dix, New Jersey. I got orders to report to Governors Island, New York, for the hearing.

I was taken to the barracks and met up with four or five other men there to testify on Murphy's behalf. We didn't say much and kept to ourselves. I think we all felt uncomfortable about why we'd been called to the base.

That afternoon a captain from the staff judge advocate's office came to talk to us. He was going to represent Murphy.

We all sat down on a couple of footlockers and the captain went over what was going to happen at the hearing.

Finally, he stopped and looked at me.

"God, you look familiar. Where could we have known each other?"

I couldn't place him, so we went on talking about Murphy's situation. All of a sudden he asked me what unit I was with in Korea and then immediately asked if I knew Vaillancourt.

"Yeah, he was my platoon sergeant."

He shot straight up and clapped his hands. I stood up and he gave me a hug.

"Did you ever give a couple of thirty-round carbine magazines to a lieutenant friend of his?"

Then it came back to me. Last time I saw this captain, he was a lieutenant and my section dug him out of a culvert in the Pusan perimeter. We stood hugging; a captain and a first sergeant. The other men didn't know what to think. He told me how one of the magazines I'd given him saved his life. He was in the culvert when he ran into a pair of North Korean soldiers. They fired just as he did. One of the North Korean bullets glanced off the magazine and hit his forehead, where he had been wounded during World War II. He spent almost a year in the hospital and then went to law school.

We talked a little about Vaillancourt and the battle at Unsan. I knew Vaillancourt was dead, but he was still listed as missing in action. That night I didn't sleep very well. Instead, I relived Pusan and Unsan. I thought about the captain, Vaillancourt and Murphy.

After all we'd been through, Murphy now had to defend himself against accusations made by unknown men. For all he or I knew the men who'd made the accusations had been the guilty ones. I hated this; it was not right. A man should be allowed to face his accusers. I knew one thing: Wherever my future took me, I would do my best to make sure men were treated justly. The way these proceedings were being handled made me feel very sad.

The next morning I was taken to the board of inquiry. It was held upstairs in a two-story wooden building near the barracks. When they called my name, I went up the stairs and entered the spartan room.

"First Sergeant Richardson reporting as ordered," I said, snapping off a smart salute.

Inside the room were seven colonels sitting behind a long wooden table. Papers and pads covered up most of the fine wood. The presiding officer, his hair cut short and flecked with gray, returned my salute. Murphy and the captain sat nearby. I tried to catch Murphy's eye, but he avoided me. He looked tired and beaten.

I was sworn in by the presiding officer, a colonel.

"Take a seat, Sergeant," he said.

The presiding officer started the questions. At first the questions dealt with me and how I knew Murphy. I remember the main question was hypothetical. If Murphy were taking a patrol into enemy territory, would I go with him?

"Murphy is a good soldier. He received the Silver Star before he was captured," I said. "However, he was an engineer and I was an infantryman. If I was taking out the patrol, I would not hesitate a minute to take Murphy with me."

The colonel smiled and made a note. There was a brief pause, then I asked a question.

"Have any of you ever been a prisoner of war?" I said, staring each officer in the eye.

A look of complete shock came over the members of the board. I don't remember what prompted me to ask the board members that question. Maybe it was out of frustration. These men knew nothing about what it took to survive three years in a prison camp. Starvation, lice and beatings. They hadn't watched their brothers die on a snowy road while sadistic guards tried to march the life out of them. They hadn't been left for dead in the morgue.

Everyone held his breath waiting for the colonel's reaction. He looked to the right and the three officers shook their heads no. He turned to the left and got the same reaction. Finally, the colonel looked at me.

"Sergeant Richardson, we got your message and thank you for your insight and appearance before the board," the colonel said.

I stood up and saluted. He returned my salute and I could

see all of the board members smiling. I did an about face and left the room.

As I walked out, I knew that nothing was ever going to intimidate me again. I'd already survived hell. I think from that day forward whenever I was faced with a tough situation I would think or in some cases say, What were they going to do, take me out in the morning and shoot me?

EPILOGUE

After Korea, I never looked back and asked why him and not me. I just accepted the idea that my life was a gift, and every day I tried to live that life the best way I knew how.

But my experiences in Korea were never far from my mind. I was never again faced with tougher decisions and I always knew that my mind was the key. It was the key to survival then and the key to overcoming every challenge afterward.

After a year as first sergeant of "G" company, 364th Infantry Regiment, I was reassigned to the regimental headquarters. The commander wanted to put me in for a direct commission, but a major in the headquarters encouraged me to go to Officers Candidate School instead.

"Bill, if you take a direct commission, you will probably be out of a job when they cut back the force," he said. "Go to Officers Candidate School, get your commission and then you will at least have a couple of years to prove yourself."

This was the best career advice I had received. So with my GED high school diploma in hand, I was off to Officers Candidate School and a career I could never have imagined. I graduated and was assigned to the 505th Airborne Infantry Regiment for five years, three of which were spent in Europe. Upon my return I was assigned to Special Forces at Fort Bragg, North Carolina.

That assignment took me all over the world and eventually

Claire and I on our wedding day, February 20, 1954.
Author's collection

into command of Project Delta in Vietnam. Created in 1964, the unit collected intelligence in remote areas. I started the unit from the ground up with the help of some very talented sergeants and officers. Project Delta still remains as the basic guide for operations deep in enemy territory.

January 19, 1957. Starting my new career as 2nd Lieutenant.

Author's collection

After Vietnam, I returned to Fort Bragg and the 82nd Airborne Division. I had the privilege to command the First Battalion of the 325th Airborne Infantry for two years. An exciting time, shared with young enthusiastic bright men. The best our country had to offer.

A number of years later I was selected for regimental command. I opted to take command of the First Corps Support Command (COSCOM), a much larger command than a regiment and what I considered to be a greater challenge. During the fifty months I commanded COSCOM we conducted operations all around the world. Our motto was "The Sun Never Sets on COSCOM." I was the last infantry officer to com-

U.S. Army War College, Carlisle, Pennsylvania, 1978. (back row): Bill III, Lynn, Mark, and Cathy. (front row): Bill Jr., Jeff, and Claire.   *Author's collection*

mand COSCOM. It would be an understatement to say that this command was a challenge.

During my thirty-nine-year career, I have had the honor of working with some of the finest soldiers and officers in the Army. Looking back, my career may have started out as a means

The other half of the photo that Wray was carrying in prison. Claire was carrying this half while I was in prison. This half has been on our refrigerator for the past fifty-seven years. *Author's collection*

to escape the streets of Philadelphia, but it ended up being a great and rewarding experience. But it would never have been anything without Claire.

Soon after coming back from Korea, I married the love of my life, my soul mate, Claire. She gave me five wonderful children and a great family life. She supported me in every way, including helping to put me through college, something I could never have accomplished without her.

Every day on this journey I believed the men of the weapons platoon and my close buddies in prison were watching me to see how I looked after my men and prepared them for whatever they may have had to face.

I tried my best to make them proud of me.

INDEX

Colonel William "Bill" Richardson, USA (Ret.) was a master sergeant with the First Cavalry Division in Korea. Commissioned in January 1957, he served eight years with the 82nd Airborne Division, and commanded the 1st BN 325th Airborne Infantry. Richardson spent seven years with Special Forces as an A-Team leader during Operation White Star in Laos, and the Cuban Missile Crisis. He was the first and third commander of Project Delta in Vietnam; attended the U.S. Army War College; and commanded the First Corps Support Command for fifty months, at which time he provided the logistical support for six thousand soldiers who invaded Grenada. As his final command, he was garrison commander at Fort Bragg, North Carolina, where he ended his thirty-nine-year career. He is currently CEO of Richardson & Sons Construction, Inc., the vice president of the Military Ex–Prisoner of War Foundation, and the former president of the 1st Cavalry Division Association. Richardson was elected to the Officer Candidate School Hall of Fame in Fort Benning, Georgia. He and his wife, Claire, have been married for fifty-six years and have five children.

Kevin Maurer is an award-winning reporter who has been embedded with the 82nd Airborne Division and U.S. Special Forces in Afghanistan.